A BERMONDSEY AND ROTHERHITHE ALBUM

Above: Jacob's Island, Bermondsey; watercolour, 1887 by James Lawson Stewart. Courtesy: Museum of London.
Immortalised by Dickens as the place where Bill Sikes ended his life in Oliver Twist, the 'island' was the slum area surrounded by water between London Street and Jacob Street.

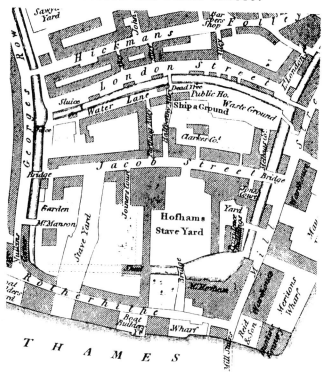

A BERMONDSEY AND ROTHERHITHE ALBUM

:a collection of nineteenth and twentieth century
picture material, photographs by Lesley McDonald,
historical notes, and descriptive, imaginative writing

compiled by
Peter Marcan

PETER MARCAN PUBLICATIONS:1992

Published 1992 by
Peter Marcan Publications,
31 Rowliff Rd,
High Wycombe, Bucks HP12 3LD

ISBN: 1 871811 06 6

Descriptive, imaginative passages by Peter Marcan, © Peter Marcan, 1992. Copyright of pictures by Geoffrey Appleton, Rose Cecil, Peter Chase, Cyril Cooke, Dennis Flanders, David Fried, Dennis Flanders, Peter Kennedy, Nathaniel Kornbluth, Paul Middleton, Martin Millard, Rachel Reckitt, Louise Soloway is owned by these artists.

Photographs of surviving points of historical and architectural interest © Lesley McDonald, 1992.

Front of cover shows old Bacon's School, Grange Road; etching of Cherry Garden Pier by Norman Janes (reproduction: courtesy of Marian Janes), and the South London Mission, Bermondsey Street, drawing by Ernest Hasseldine, 1932.
Back of cover shows St Mary's Rotherhithe, wood engraving by Rachel Reckitt, 1949.

I acknowledge with thanks the British Library (Newspaper Division) for authorising reproduction of photocopies of periodical illustrations, and the Local Studies Library, London Borough of Southwark for authorising reproduction of photocopies of items held in their collections.
It has not proved possible to trace the executors, or next of kin of William Washington, or Barclay Baron. Should this publication come to their attention, they are requested to contact the publisher to negotiate any relevant fees.

Printed and bound by Short Run Press Ltd, Exeter.

CONTENTS

BERMONDSEY:

Impressions of Bermondsey 1-4
Tower Bridge, and Tower Bridge Road 5-9
Gardens, playgrounds and open spaces in
   Bermondsey 10
Bermondsey's leather industry 11-13
Tooley Street 14-22
Tanner Street 23-27
In and around Snowsfields 28-29
Bermondsey Street 29-36
Decima Street 37
Spa Road 38-39
Grange Walk, The Grange and Grange Road 40-43
Long Lane 44-45
Abbey Street 46-48
Butlers Wharf 48
Jacob Street 49
The Circle, Queen Elizabeth Street 50
Dockhead 51-53
Bermondsey Wall, Farncombe Street, George Row 54-56
Doctor Salter at Cherry Garden Pier 57
Cambridge University Mission, Bermondsey
   Settlement 58-59
South Bermondsey 60-62
West Lane 63
Southwark Park 64-65

ROTHERHITHE:

Central Rotherhithe and Rotherhithe Street 66-67
Vistas of Rotherhithe 68-70
Churches, old and new 71
St Helena Gardens 72
Rotherhithe Tunnel 73
Rotherhithe Street and environs 74-82
Greenland Dock and Surrey Quays area 83-88
Lower Road 83, 89-93
Bibliography of books and articles on
   Bermondsey and Rotherhithe for further
   reading 94-95
Notes on artists, and sculptors featured 96-100
Adverts 101

IMPRESSIONS OF BERMONDSEY

Peter Marcan came to Bermondsey in 1991, finding a place of refuge here; coming from across the river, he longed for a different environment, and for just a little more peacefulness. He writes:-

Bermondsey is perhaps surprisingly a place of towers and turrets, of spires and extraordinary chimneys. Perhaps only from Bermondsey does Tower Bridge look so enticing and magical. In Bermondsey Square the clinical precision of the tower block of Guys Hospital on the horizon glares out at the tender gracefulness of St Mary's Church. In Tower Bridge Road the monumental chimney of the old jam factory Hartleys confronts the slender spire of Haddon Hall Baptist Church. Bermondsey is also a place of boredom and anxiety, a place where many are unemployed, where so often there seems to be nothing at all to do; a place beneath the Thames at high tide, which feels too much like a backwater. In Bermondsey one must make daily attempts to find stimulation: reading the Bible, plunging into newspapers, drinking strong black coffee, mad violin playing sessions, writing letters to get letters back, reading, dreaming, trying to feel at home at home. This is a place where daily efforts must be made to jerk oneself out of boredom. And yet all sorts and types of people can be found here living, studying, plying their trades and professions. Traffic pours down Tower Bridge Road relentlessly on weekday afternoons. People from all over London and perhaps the world get down here on Friday mornings for the Antiques Market. Guys Hospital, London Bridge, Southwark Cathedral, the Tower of London: all landmarks just outside this place remind us that however inert we may have become, the great world is on our doorstep. There is anxiety too: anxiety about a place which once hummed with industry: Christy's the hatters, Martin's the fur merchants, Cross & Blackwell's pickles in Crimscott St, Jacob's biscuits in Wolseley St, Messrs Peek Freans in Drummond Rd were all once here; long gone, very long time ago, is Bermondsey Abbey flattened into oblivion beneath the car park, jeered at by the advertising hoardings, forgotten by the bric-a-brac dealers on Friday mornings. Pore over the London A-Z and you will spot many street names reminding us of much that has disappeared. The mind reels at the thought of all the life that this place has seen, reels and then sinks into a kind of bemused numbness.

Simon Hughes is Bermondsey's Social & Liberal Democrat M.P. The following article 'Out of the cupboard' was contributed to the Evening Standard's 'Why I live in...' series in their issue of 29th August 1990. It is reproduced courtesy of Simon Hughes.

I came here for work. It was very simple really. When I started as a pupil barrister - in the old days, when you got no income at all - I needed to live somewhere within cycling distance of the Temple and in the cheapest accommodation I could find.

There were three of us in the same straits. Starting a career with no money, we scoured inner London for somewhere suitable to live. We used to go out looking in an old Austin A40, a bicycle strapped on the top. We would park the car, take off the bike and the three of us would do concentric circles - one on foot, one on two wheels and one on four - looking for possible homes.

But, in the end, shelter came from another direction. An old friend from college had moved to London to run a youth organisation in North Camberwell. They wanted youth workers and offered accommodation over the shop.

So the three of us moved into a very cheap flat in a solid old vicarage, just a few yards off the Old Kent Road. I stayed there for six years while undergoing my indoctrination in how to be "streetwise" in the inner city in the 1970s. Kids on the run from the police, kids trying to beat up their parents or kids trying to beat up - and in one or two cases kill - eath other were the regular fare. Real hard community politics did not take long to learn. But when I got heavily into party politics, I had to give up the youth work, so they threw me out. A friend put me up and I lived in what was all but a cupboard.

Indeed, when I was selected as a candidate for Bermondsey I was still living in the cupboard. Desparately I searched the constituency for somewhere just slightly more secure. It was very hard to find anywhere to rent, let alone buy in Bermondsey, with owner-occupation at 2.2 per cent and 80 per cent of all property owned by the council - I think there was a total of six properties for sale!

We found one which had the appealing features of a kitchen extension with sliding patio doors, a little garden and a sauna in the basement. There were a few snags: we discovered the kitchen extension had not been given planning permission; the sauna was there because it had been a "private club" with a dubious history; and a garden full of cannabis.

Negotiations broke down when the owner got locked up - but I suppose that's par for the course in a constituency where many more than the average number of people go away for unintended holidays as guests of Her Majesty.

At last I found an upstairs maisonette for sale in Lynton Road, just the other side of the Old Kent Road and almost immediately behind the Dun Cow. It is in an area that was beautified in the Twenties when one of my illustrious predecessors Dr Salter, and his progressive wife Ada, realised that one of the best ways to improve the health of the people was to improve their environment. They planted trees in each road as well as building the first council houses (and municipal sauna) and did lots of other good things, the legacy of which is still with us in the physical layout of Bermondsey today.

I moved into the top half of the house but it wasn't long before the bottom half came up for sale (if you were living below a General Election campaign wouldn't you move?) People often say to me as I go about my business: "You don't know what it's like", when they are talking about the lack of rubbish collection, or the squatters next door. I think I do. My place is at the end of a small terrace. The rest of the terrace was falling down, then empty, then squatted, and only just now, after seven years, has been done up and occupied.

Behind me there were derelict council sheds with inglorious corrugated iron, squatted by that least quiet of neighbours, a car-body repair shop. One night I woke up thinking: isn't it noisy? Isn't it light? Isn't it warm? And then realised the building next door was ablaze and flames were licking the side of my home. Just another arson attack.

Then they decided to demolish the haulage yard opposite. Sitting in my little garden one sunny summer's afternoon, with band rehearsal on one side, panel-beating on the other, demolition opposite and a plane flying overhead, I thought: inner-city life? This is what it's all about.

And now even my haven - my little garden - has been under attack. One morning a couple of weeks ago I was in the shower when the contractor, working for the local council which had decided to replace the corrugated iron shed by a local housing office, suddenly demolished my garden wall.

By accident of course ... even more accidental than the council decision to put a housing office next to me. "If you're not satisfied with what we are doing you know where you can go." Next door. As soon as they open, I'll be first in the queue.

But in spite of all this, and the fact that the local form of exchange and mart means I have increasingly to make the place look like Fort Knox, it is a good place to be - a real community with real live community politics to get involved with.

There are the battles to increase low-cost housing for those who want to rent or buy against the pressure to price everything out of the range of 99 per cent of locals; the battles to make sure the regeneration of Docklands is conservation and not destruction of all the community holds dear; the battle to force the Government to commit itself to give us the Bermondsey Tube station on the Jubilee Line (I will certainly throw a political fit if we don't).

It is all very well other people writing about how wonderful their area is, but ours holds not only some of the best of old London and the best of the new, it was once London's throbbing and working heart. And if you look at the map it is the centre still.

Above: Bombed out Bermondsey, a conte crayon drawing by Ethel Gabain, 1941. Courtesy: South London Art Gallery.

The following illustrated article 'Down here in Bermondsey' by 'a resident' appeared in the Daily Express, 4th May, 1929:

If you enter Tower Bridge road from the Old Kent road you will find yourself in Bermondsey.

You will smell smells from fish stalls and old clothes barrows ... from jellied eel shops that have basins of grey liquid in the windows, with fat sausages and meat pies alongside them.

You will find fish and chip saloons, with clouds of hot fishy vapour curling out of the doors, and red posters in the windows advertising the programmes at the local picture palace. Great warehouses, factories, and blocks of tenements loom up all round.

In spite of this Bermondsey has a spell. The people who live within its bounds are as unsnobbish as the fisherfolk in a Donegal coast hamlet.

Bermondsey square, where I live, is the site of old Bermondsey Abbey. And they say it rivalled Westminster itself in the days before the Dissolution. Foundries, tan yards, and various public works surround Bermondsey square now.

At the very gates of the old abbey, too, there is now a building called the Great Central Hall, with swing doors and a grand organ. It is owned by the South London Mission, and in it they sing Wesleyan hymns with gusto every Sunday night.

Look down any side street off Tower Bridge road, and you are likely to see a draggled man walking slowly in the middle of the road and trying to sing.

He looks expectantly up at the windows; then you hear a copper jingling down on the road, and the old fellow ambles off, breaking his song, to pick it up.

You may see another of the sorrowful brotherhood with a barrel organ, and children gathered round lilting and dancing to the music. The man growls at them to go away, for they distract the attention of potential almsgivers from himself.

Sunday is visiting day in Bermondsey. Relatives come to tea, and a social evening with the gramophone, or community singing, is the rule.

The music is not highbrow. The songs are nearly always "wondering" songs, and about "caring" and "remembering" and "pals" and "wonderful girls".

They sing the same ones over and over again.

Sometimes, especially when beer has formed part of the entertainment, shrill voices are raised in argument, and the noise of breaking crockery mars the conviviality, but that is nothing - in Bermondsey.

(Reproduction: courtesy of the Daily Express)

Above: a drawing from Bermondsey Walk, London Borough of Southwark, 1984. Courtesy: London Borough of Southwark.

TOWER BRIDGE

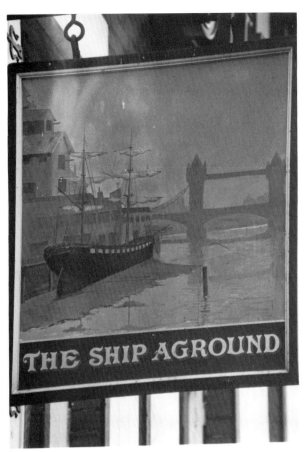

Above: The Ship Aground pub, 33 Wolseley St. Another pub with the same name stood here until demolished in 1907 (drawn by J. Appleton, J.R. Emslie and R.J. Angel).

Above: A lino cut by Helen Ziegler.

Above: The Rising Sun pub, Old Jamaica Rd.

Opposite: An illustration by Ernest Hasseldine from The Glory in the garret, Epworth Press, 1932.

TOWER BRIDGE ROAD

The approach to Bermondsey is by way of London's grandest bridges. Tower Bridge can often be glimpsed from streets in Bermondsey, its turrets glistening jewel-like in the sun. It is an entrance and an exit and reminds us strongly of our more optimistic past: a monument on the list to be ticked off, or to linger on if you come here as a tourist; a place for stimulation when one is bored; a bridge to hurry across if you are fleeing from your work place, but it must be crossed if one is to penetrate Bermondsey.

Once over the bridge, the road sinks down, quickly leaving behind the tension of the metropolis, sinking down into the northern reaches of South London. Tourists often wander on for a short distance, maybe they reach the Cat and Cucumber Cafe on the corner of Druid Street, but they feel they are now on alien territory and turn back. Tower Bridge Road leads us past Sarson's Vinegar Works (recently closed), the old National Leathersellers College, 1910, opposite, past large antiques warehouses, and council estates. At the cross road it changes its nature and becomes a fairly typical London high street with its assorted jumble of shops and pubs. The Pagoda pub on the corner of the renovated Brighton Buildings of 1892 brings a touch of originality to this stretch of Tower Bridge Road. In the late 1980's trendy new businesses set up here on the ground floor of Brighton Buildings; here were Yum Yum (children's wear), Pretty Steps (exclusive Italian and Spanish shoes), and Curiosity (cards and gifts); today, in our recessionary climate, they are closing down.

At the cross roads we reach a great territorial division: we know that here the Bermondsey corner of the world ends: the Old Kent Road leads down to New Cross, the New Kent Road to the Elephant and Castle.

TOOLEY STREET

Tooley Street, by way of contrast, is a street of imposing edifices, reminding us that the powers that be are close at hand: at the junction with Tower Bridge Road one finds a police station and magistrates court with a branch of the National Westminster Bank, of 1900, opposite. Samuel Bevington, the first mayor of Bermondsey surveys the street from his plinth, beside the bust of Ernest Bevin, the labour leader. Two grandiose pubs the King of Belgium, and St John's Tavern St stand opposite one another at the entrance to Tooley Street Gardens. Smaller pubs present themselves as one progresses down the street: The Antigallician on the corner of Vine Lane, the disused Britannia, 1881, and the Duke of Clarence on the corner of Battle Bridge Lane. This is also a street where the contemporary world asserts itself: in Magdalen House a company Positive Images tell us on its windows that it has its fingers in many pies: it offers business communications, design, exhibitions, conferences, and video. Under the arches we encounter a bicycle shop (On Your Bike), the Bow Tie Sandwich Bar, and the London Dungeon, which offers us 'Degradation, damnation, death'. We are living in a strange world.

The opposite side of the road offers us perhaps more reassurance with its imposing architecture of another age: the old fire station, the old warehouse building of Board & Co, the reconstructed Hay's Dock warehouses, and the strikingly ornamented Denmark House.

BERMONDSEY TOWERS AND TURRETS

Opposite: A drawing by Ernest Hasseldine from The Glory in the garret, Epworth Press, 1932. The market no longer extends to the mission.

Above: The Tabard Centre, part of Southwark's Adult Education Institute; previously a London School Board school, built 1873.

Above: Turret of the Pagoda pub, Tower Bridge Road.

Above: Turret of the disused Tower Hotel, built 1897, architect W.A. Withall.

Above: St John's, Horsleydown, built 1724, architects Hawksmoor and John James; drawn by C. Burton. Bombed, its foundations were used for a new building Nasmith House, 1972-6 (London City Mission).

Opposite: The early 18th century vicarage of the old church. A plaque on the wall records that Thomas Guy (1644-1724) was born nearby at 7, Pritchard Alley.

GARDENS, PLAYGROUNDS AND OPEN SPACES IN BERMONDSEY

I walked to the Tanner Street playground one summers day to sit there and read on my way home from the West End: a hidden patch of open space with its tied up swings, tennis courts and a relic of the old St Olave's Church tucked away in one corner. The tennis players present a curious spectacle: athletic types spring hither and thither; schoolgirls know they are quite useless; students are keen to keep fit; a father comes in with his basket of green balls and tiny offspring; he taps the balls gently at them across the nets; their rackets are almost as big as they are. A gang of kids with their out-of-work father comes in to kick a ball about; the little girls go off into the bushes and yank out an executives case; they all swoop on it like greedy little vultures; they pull out all the stuff; was this an executive so despairing of his lot that he simply threw it all away? Simply vanished and never went home again? But today, as the afternoon reaches its peak, the park feels no concern for such brooding matters; two spaniels frolic around, the inner city sparrows hop and flit; many people are away, the student year has closed. I sat here, late one afternoon and read a biographical account of an artist's life: lived out in London in the 1940's and 1950's: full of turbulence and anxiety, of endless crazy goings on, of unsatisfied desires, of excessive sociability, and loneliness, and work commissions pouring in all the time; but now the park was emptied completely; a flag flutters over Turtle & Pearce, banner makers since 1872; but everything has now gone very still...

Then there is another space called Leathermarket Gardens: the haunt of delirious drunks, of people housed in the broken down old estate nearby (renovated, in fact, at a later stage); the red and cream roses are small and stunted; the wooden seats are stuck in holly bushes; grafitti litters the wooden shelter; a broken down old couple sits there hugging one another tightly; grown weary with nothingness, they sink ever further into forgetfulness; a park full of red and cream roses; yet seedy and unloved...I must move on...

Away from all this, eastwards and much closer to English normality is Bermondsey Spa Gardens; wooden tables and seats are there for picnics; a blackbird bounces about; pigeons think about nothing; fathers take their toddlers for a stroll, youths puff at their cigarettes; surrounded by printing works, an old Victorian school, two pubs (The Grange and The Queen's Arms), the old 1891 public library, the 1930's council offices, the new Alaska business complex, life in Bermondsey Spa Gardens asks no questions and poses no threats.

Potters Field Park in Tooley Street opposite the grandiose King of Belgium pub is yet again another kind of open space in Bermondsey. This is a park which has been extended recently - opening up access to the riverside (where Pickle Herring Street previously ran) opposite the Tower of London, and to the Butlers Wharf riverside walk on the other side of the Tower Bridge. One can come to Tooley Street Gardens to gawp at these monuments or else to savour the humanity to be found here. Down and outs hold out their hands to all and sundry; they beg for pennies; what do the city gents have to say to them? one even managed to scrounge a sandwich off me. Never-ending tourists, in groups, whole gangs, couples, families all stroll through here; they must be many miles away from home; what do they see here? what will they remember about this place? And the city folk: what are they thinking of, as they strut along bolt upright; groups of young men who are making it, solitary university graduates just starting in the city, executives with their secretaries; people from Southwark crown court, all pass to and fro here, office workers tired out by a morning's futility come here to puff at a cigarette, and escape into a book. I too often sit there munching my lunch-time sandwiches, fed up with my morning efforts, feeling distracted, wondering about my future, wondering who on earth is going to come around the corner next; but this is certainly not a lunch-time parade of Bermondsey folk.

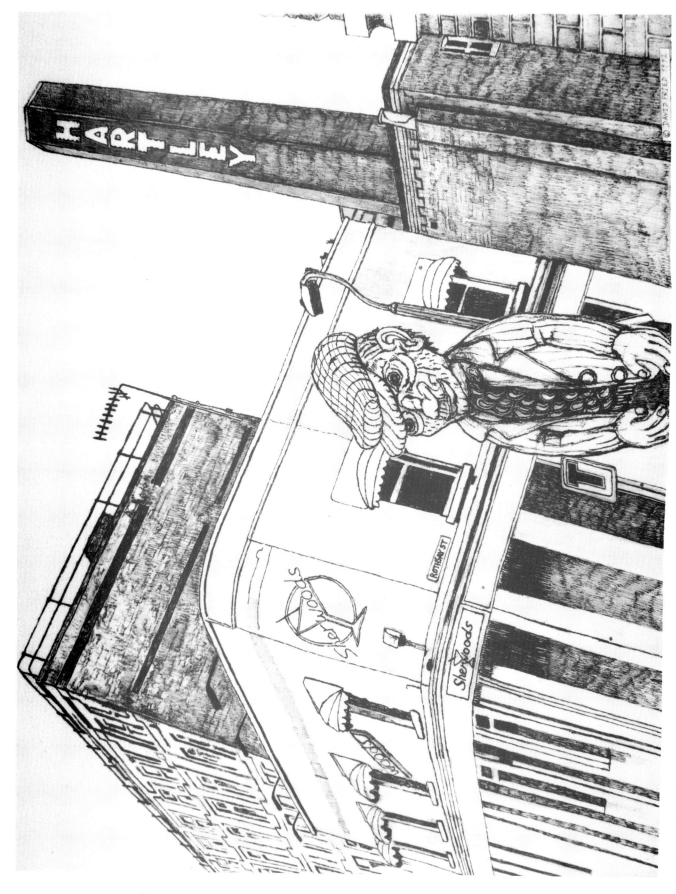

Hartley, the jam factory (now closed down) is a hugue, rambling factory block built in 1901. It has impressive entrance gates, and is dominated by a large chimney as shown in David Fried's drawing. The cloth-capped figure stares uneasily within himself. Does he recall more prosperous times in

BERMONDSEY'S LEATHER INDUSTRY COMMEMORATED IN PUB SIGNS

Above: Leather Exchange pub, 15, Leathermarket St. (May be changing its name to the Juggler's Arms).

Above: Tanners Arms, 60 Willow Walk.

Above: Simon the Tanner, 231 Long Lane (replaced recently with new sign).

Above: The Bermondsey leather and skin market.

Above: The London Leather Exchange, architects George Elkington; an engraving from the Builder, 1879. It ceased functioning as a centre for buying and selling about 1912; currently disused, but an important reminder of Bermondsey's past.
The adjacent leather market in Weston Street was established in 1833.

Scenes from Bermondsey leather-making: relief sculptures on wall of the old Leather Exchange, Leathermarket Street/Weston Street.

TOOLEY STREET

Above: Magistrates Court, Tooley Street, built 1904, architect J.D. Butler. To be contrasted with the somewhat dull, functional Crown Court, built 1979-82, P.S.A. Architects, in English Grounds (opposite HMS Belfast).

Opposite: A drawing from Southwark Annual, 1899 of the public Institute in Fair St, architects Stock, Page and Stock. The facilities included a gymnasium, library and large hall.

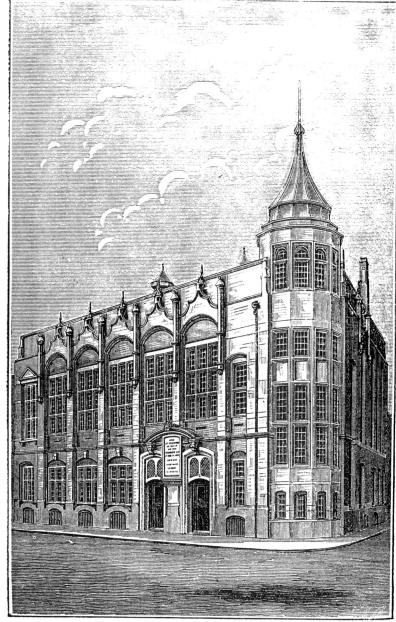

Above: Former offices of the St Olave's Union in Tooley Street, architect Newman and Newman; a drawing from the London Argus, 1899; later occupied by London Borough of Southwark Social Services; currently disused(?)

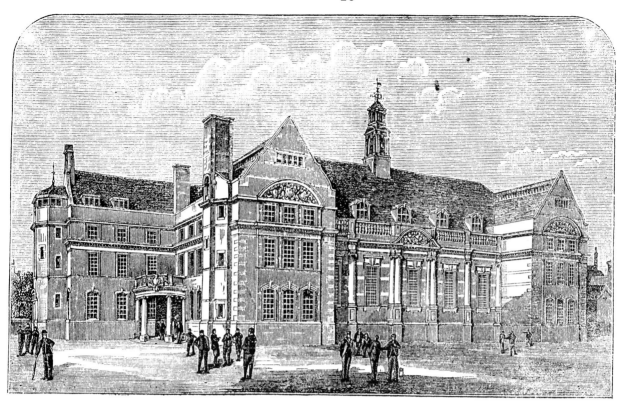

Above: An engraving from the Southwark Annual, 1894, of the old St Olave's Grammar School, Tooley Street, built 1893, architect E.W. Mountford; now Tower Bridge branch of the South London College. The central frieze shows two schoolboys, one with book, the other with cricket bat.

Above: King of Belgium pub, 1897, Tooley St.

Above: Statue to Samuel Bourne Bevington, by Sydney Marsh; behind is the bust of the labour leader Ernest Bevin.

Above: South view of Queen Elizabeth's Free Grammar School in Tooley Street; a drawing by R.B. Schnebbelie, engraved by Wise, 1813. St Olave's Grammar School, founded by Queen Elizabeth I occupied buildings shown in this attractive print until 1830 when they were demolished to make way for the new railway. Another building occupied a site in Bermondsey Street, demolished in 1849; the school subsequently moved to the eastern end of Tooley St. The building now standing was erected in 1892-95, and occupied from 1896 until 1968.

The shot tower in the background was erected in 1808 for manufacturing bullets (molten lead was dropped into water from it). It was destroyed during Topping's Wharf fire in 1843, together with St Olave's Church (shown in right hand corner).

Above: The Tooley Street front of warehouse (which once stretched down to the river) premises of distillers Messrs Board & Co.

Above: Disi Lisi Teapots – a stall in Hays Galleria.

Opposite: A hostel for down and outs in Tooley Street; a drawing by Martin Millard, 1991.

Opposite: A fire in Tooley Street; an engraving from the Illustrated London News, 1851.

Above: The Navigators, kinetic sculpture by David Kemp in Hay's Galleria. In the background is a branch of the wine merchants Balls Bros.

SOME OVERLOOKED ARTISTIC DETAIL IN TOOLEY STREET

Opposite: Detail from the ornamental western front of Denmark House, 15 Tooley St, designed by S.D. Adshed in 1908 for the Bennett Steamship Company, and now part of the private London Bridge Hospital.

Above: Shipwrights Arms, on corner of Bermondsey Street.

Above: Black and gold mosaic by Colin Gill of St Olave on side of Tooley Street entrance to St Olaf House, designed by H.S. Goodhart-Rendel in 1931 as the headquarters of the Hays Wharf Company.

Above: An engraving by William Washington. Reproduction: courtesy of Guildhall Library. The demolished church dates from 1740 when the old church was rebuilt. The turret has been preserved in a corner of the playground in Tanner Street.

TANNER STREET

This strange, historical curiosity is tucked away in the corner of Tanner Street playground. It is all that was preserved of St Olave's Church when demolished in 1928. The site originally was part of vegetable gardens and orchards of the Abbey, later pasture land attached to the farm on Sir Thomas Pope's estate, then market gardens, later in the second half of the 19th century and early 20th century the site of St Olave's workhouse, demolished in 1925.

© DAVID FRIED 1992

Above: Coopers Arms Tavern: a watercolour drawing by T.H. Shepherd, 1854. (from the Crace Collection, British Museum). Courtesy: Trustees of the British Museum.

Above: A drawing by Martin Millard, 1991 showing the Tower Bridge end of Tanner Street with Sarson's vinegar vats. Sarson's have recently closed their works and this view may well vanish in time.
Another, very different, rendering of the same subject is Vincent Driscoll's oil painting 'Midsummer night'.

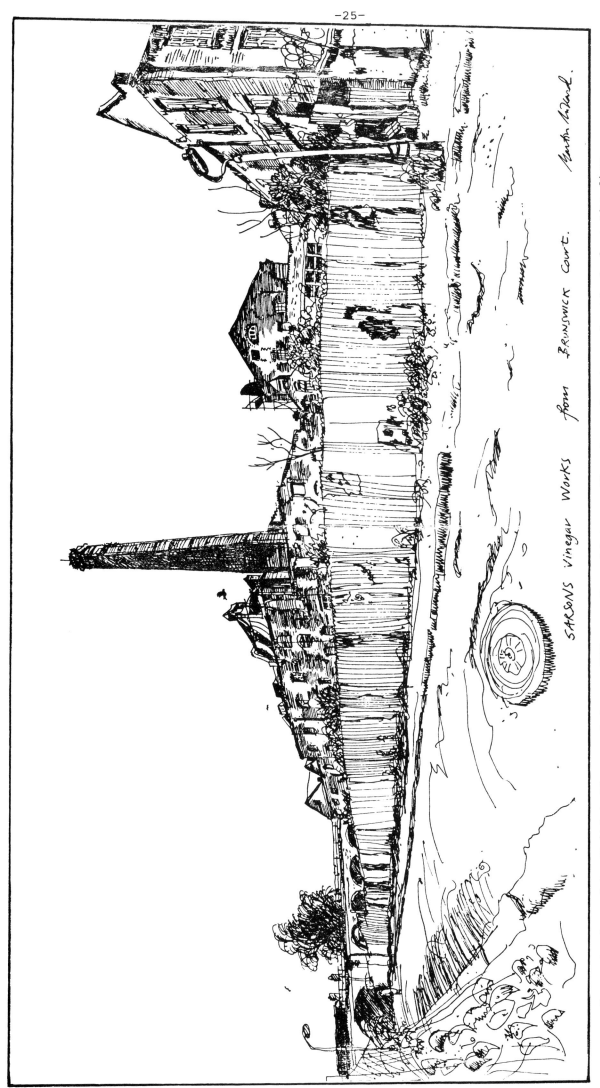

SARSONS Vinegar Works from BRUNSWICK Court.

Sarson's (owned by British Vinegars) has a 200 year long history. The above drawing, shortly before the firm announced its closure, by Martin Millard, 1992, shows the rear of the building from a side street off Tanner St.

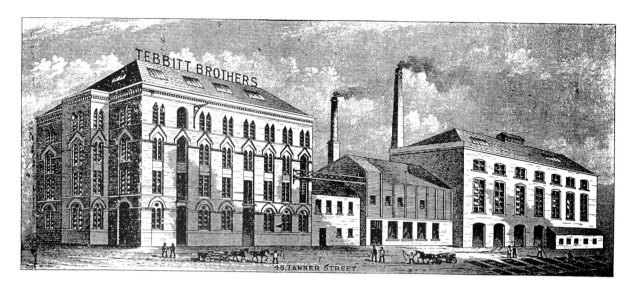

Above: An engraving of Messrs Tebbitt Bros' Leather manufactory, 48 Tanner Street; from A Descriptive Account of Southwark & Bermondsey, W.T. Pike, 1894; works established in 1867.

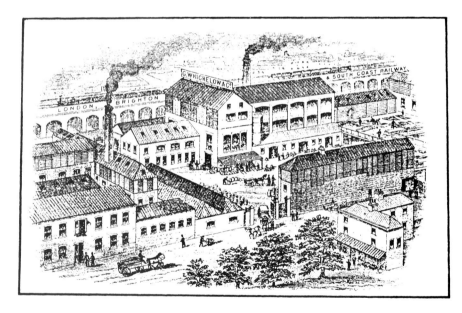

Above: An engraving of Mr G Whichelow's Leather manufactory, Tidal Place, Tanner Street; from A Descriptive Account of Southwark & Bermondsey, W.T. Pike, 1894; works established in 1865.

Above: Watercolour drawing of Sarson's Vinegar Factory, Tower Bridge Road, 1979, by Cyril Cooke. Courtesy: South London Art Gallery.

IN AND AROUND SNOWSFIELDS

Above: Rose pub sign, on corner of Snowsfields and Weston Street.

Above: Guiness Trust Buildings, 1898, Snowsfields opposite the old Arthur's Mission.

Above: The Horseshoe Inn, 1897, at the bottom of Melior St.

IN AND AROUND SNOWSFIELDS

If Bermondsey Street conveys the bustle and stampede of present day business life, the area around Snowsfields suggests a quieter more domestic mood. People put down their roots, one feels, in the three blocks of the Guiness Trust Buildings: its wrought iron railings and friezes grace and protect this place lovingly. The Rose and The Horseshoe Inn provide places for intimate meetings; the Manna Centre in Melior Street provides food and comfort for down and outs, and more religion is at hand in the Roman Catholic Our Lady of La Salette, and at the Pentecostal Gospel Chapel in the old Arthur's Mission building.
Dwarfing all these intimate places, to our dismay perhaps, we discover here too the City Banking College. Money pursues us wherever we stray...

BERMONDSEY STREET

Bermondsey Street by way of contrast is a very muddled street: old and new buildings jostle one another: warehouses, corner shops, cafes, pubs, a barbers, private residences, businesses of various kinds are here; some thriving, some closing down, some starting up; all kinds of people march up and down this street: a self contained, cocooned street, approached through a long tunnel at its northern end and ending with a row of trees, the Hand and Marigold pub and the South London Mission at its other end, it is a street which seems to be puzzled about its own identity, so confused has it become today. People rush away after business hours; by half past six in the evening the street has emptied; it sinks into silence and broods uneasily on all that it has seen.
Passers by may wonder about the South London Mission and what goes on there; here in this turn of the century old mission hall much community work for the needy and disadvantaged still goes on today. A variety of people do actually live here: old ladies sit out in the sun in the central courtyard: one caresses a green apple and shuts her eyes, one waters the potted plants. Students wonder whether they will scrape through their exams; private fears and longings are felt behind private doors at the South London Mission. A young lay preacher, who lived there, bored with telling sermons (he has written some 100 of them) decided one Sunday to tell the congregation his life story instead: the day his father walked out and away, how he heard about the Gospel and Jesus Christ when a teenager, his jobs selling washing machines, as a grave-digger, a cook and bottle washer in a house run by the Carr-Gomm Society, and as a bus driver, about black puddings in Bury where he comes from, and pie and mash in Bermondsey where he is now. This is a place of Christian idealism and bafflement, a place of high hopes and discoveries and of disillusionment, of lives beginning, and lives slowly ending.
At its lower end Bermondsey Street becomes Antiques Land. Almost every weekday vans of stuff come and go - all kinds of tables and chairs, ornaments, mirrors, candlesticks are carried to and fro. Bored youths hang around in doorways waiting for the next delivery. Wheeler dealers come down to snap up bargains, to engage in one-upmanship. One hot summer day even a stuffed lion appeared dumped onto the pavement to startle passers by. Antiques stuff of all kinds comes down to Bermondsey, to haggle over, to be inspected for authenticity, to be carried about, turned into money, to be resold, and then resold, to end up nobody really knows where.

BERMONDSEY STREET

Above: A drawing of ancient houses in Bermondsey Street by J. Crowther; from Lost London: being a description of landmarks which have since disappeared, pictured by J. Crowther, c. 1879-87, also described by E. Beresford Chancellor.

Above: 139, Bermondsey Street, premises of Rankin Bros & Son (corkwood growers, and importers).

Above: A drawing by Martin Millard, 1992 of the old smithy building, top of Moroco St.

ST MARY'S CHURCHYARD

This is a most curious churchyard: romantic, yet tame; mysterious, yet prosaic; many of the tomb stones have vanished from view: shrouded in wild ivy growths they have vanished completely; weather has eroded many of the inscriptions elsewhere: people buried here have slipped away now into oblivion; nobody remembers these people any more. This is a very ancient burial plot. At night time the trees rustle secretly: only they know of everything that has gone on on this plot of earth... But this is no film script churchyard preserved for Dickens adaptations: down and outs sit out their days here, couples sprawl on the lawns in the sun, wedding groups are photographed here, engineers, designers, doctors, antique dealers all pass through here; a violin student studies his scores; people come into this churchyard to ponder on everything, or on nothing at all; one by one they get up and depart; the pigeons swoop down on crumbs...

Then, one hot Sunday afternoon when I was sitting there alone, the decorator from Battersea appeared, asked me what I was doing there with my music, sat down and told me he knew all about Bermondsey. "A very strange park this," he said, "strange, strange people come here; this isn't a nice place, you be careful," he warned; "I've seen people robbed and beaten up here; in broad daylight too, and nobody raises a finger; two yobos nicked an old lady's handbag here, I saw it happen, chased them up Tower Bridge Road. This place is full of thieves, he warned, all they want is your money; or else they're on skag, do you know what that is?" Who was the decorator from Battersea? Why had he walked all the way here? "I lived here for 15 years he said. You meet all types of people here. See the council flats over there? they're full of unemployed people, people who have got nothing." "What do they do all day long," I asked. "They sleep, get up, talk to their neighbours, go to the pub, read a newspaper, eat, sleep... and then the same the next day, and the next; their kids will be like that too." "And what do they think of the business people around here? are they jealous?" I asked. "No, they're not jealous, they look up to them, see, they respect them because they go off to work, wear smart suits, run businesses. Then, there are people with money, people who live in posh places - in Bermondsey Street, in Grange Walk." I'm tired, I'm tired, said the decorator from Battersea; I've got blisters on my feet, I've been walking miles. I could tell you stories, I know so many stories..."

Above: A drawing by Martin Millard showing St Mary's churchyard, and end of Bermondsey Street.

Above: The Time and Talents Association, a remarkable Christian community organisation, was operating from this building from 1899 to 1961. The original building, an old tailors' shop, was rebuilt in 1907.

Above: Memorial in St Mary's Churchyard to James Buckingham Bevington, father of Samuel Bevington.

Above: The early nineteenth century watchhouse on the corner of Abbey Street and Bermondsey Street. At one time in the 1920's it was in use as a laundry office. On the Abbey Street side there is a disused drinking fountain dated 1859 and inscribed 'the gift of Henry Sterry'.

Bermondsey Antiques Market, Bermondsey Square: three drawings by Louise Soloway, 1992. Known historically as the New Caledonian Market, trade was conducted originally in Islington (close to the Caledonian Road) until the Second World War.

BERMONDSEY SQUARE in 1866, formerly called the COURT YARD, and originally the principal quadrangle of Bermondsey Abbey. Upon looking forward the Old Church is seen in the distance, whilst about midway on the spot now occupied by the Five Bells Public House, stood the Chapel erected in 1699 of Mr Mauduit, one of the Puritan Divines, this Chapel was afterwards a Woolwarehouse, and finally pulled down. At the opening to the Square, between the Kings John's Head Public House and the Oilshop, stood the North or great GateHouse of the Abbey, demolished about 1807, at the back of the houses on the left, in a Builders Yard, Remains of Old Walls are to be seen. On the far corner to the right is seen the entrance to the Long Walk, here in excavating for a sewer a few years since, was discovered a stone coffin, still to be seen in the vaults of the Parish Church. Midway between the entrance to the Long Walk, and the Salt Warehouse, stood the Mansion House, which old Stowe tells us was a goodly house builded of wood and stone, the materials for which being taken from the Abbey. Turning round by the Saltwarehouse, we reach the Grange Walk, here even at the present time is to be seen the East Gate House, together with the hinges upon which the gates hung, this with a few Old Houses in Bear Yard are the only remains now to be seen of this once famous Abbey.

Opposite: A watercolour drawing by T.H. Shepherd, 1853 of Bermondsey House, (Sir Thomas Pope's house), near Grange Road, built 1541 from remains of the Abbey. Courtesy: Trustees of the British Museum.

Below: Two engravings (from the London Argus, 1902), of Abbey House, 1826, adjacent to St Mary's Church. The lamb over the summer house may signify that one of the owners of the house had been a wool merchant.

Above: An illustration by Ernest Hasseldine from the South London Mission 1920 annual report 'God's lighthouse'.

Above: An illustration by Ernest Hasseldine from the South London Mission 1921 annual report 'A door of hope'.

BERMONDSEY SIDE STREET: DECIMA STREET

Decima Club Chapel

Opposite: An illustration from The Doctor, by Barclay Baron, Edward Arnold, 1952. This club, attached to the Oxford Medical Mission was at 38, Decima Street from about 1905-20.

Leading off the bottom end of Bermondsey St is Decima St - a side turning of no interest, just like any other all over London, you may say; on the corner: The Top Quality Fish and Hamburger Bar, a branch of the Handf Group offering housing and finance, and a launderette. Yet, at weekdays this street is full of humanity, full of people on business and doings; from four o'clock in the afternoon onwards endless vans pass through here: removal firms, plumbers, electricians, all kinds of building services, security services, printers, roofing contractors, pest control services; there is no end to the self-employed people here offering specialist services. People doing business with printers pass through here, coming from elsewhere in London and the country; there are medical students intent on their futures, school teachers, social workers, people coming to the job club.
 At weekends the street goes very quiet; kids play about with nothing to do, dogs are walked, bored youths trot home with their rented videos, or bottles of booze. Children come to visit their ageing parents, sit about on sofas, wonder where life is; people lean over their balconies, stare into space, try to figure out what life is all about; but nobody can really know what goes on within the rooms of these hugue council estates. Many people probably find a refuge here: indeed tucked away up crumbling staircases, one may find extraordinary people: a distinguished scholar and translator of Russian twentieth century poetry; perhaps artists creating vast panoramas of a nation in its death throes before the turn of the millenium, inventors of genius, brilliant pop musicians, dreaming of stardom, who knows, who knows?

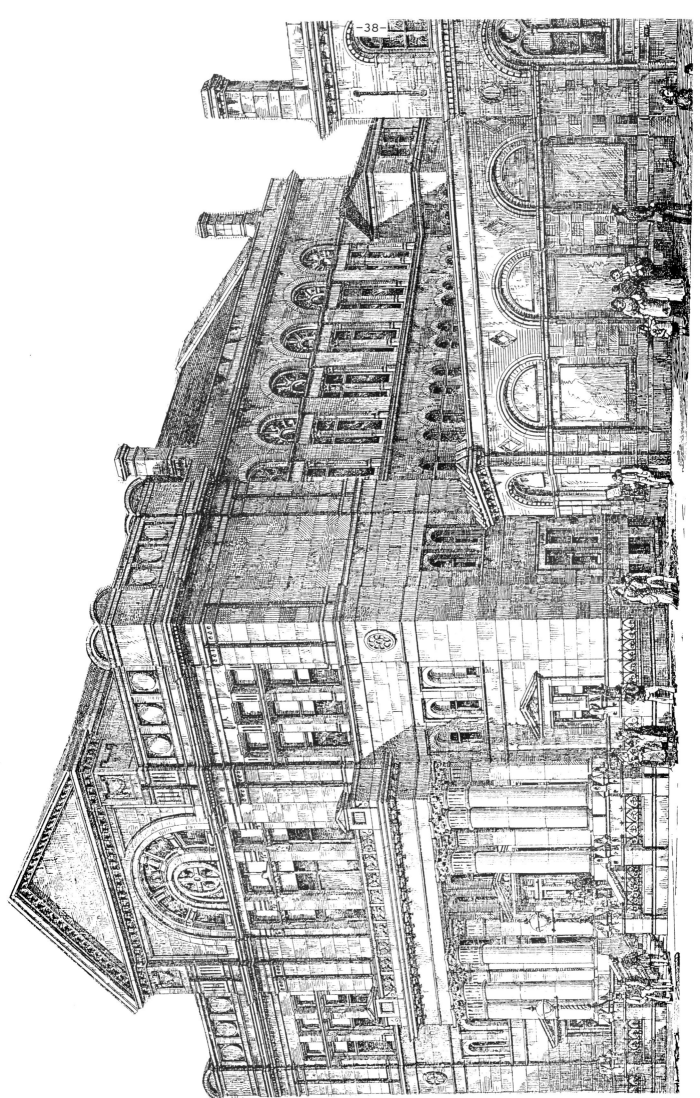

Above: An engraving of Bermondsey Town Hall, Spa Rd (destroyed by bombing), architects Elkington & Sons, from the Builder, 1880.

SPA ROAD

Above: Bermondsey baths and washhouse, opened in 1854, the first of their kind in London; adjacent to the town hall, both now demolished; new baths opened in 1927 in Grange Road.

Above: Old Bermondsey Central Library, built 1890, architect John Johnson.

Above: Council offices, built 1928, architect H. Tansley. Note the Borough of Bermondsey coat of arms on the pediment.

GRANGE WALK

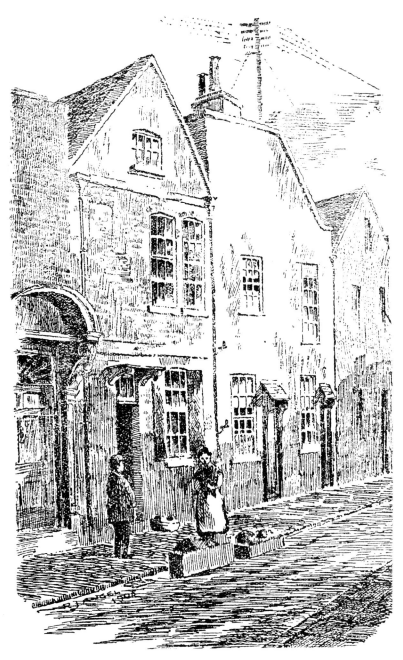

Above: A drawing by R.J. Angel showing the hinges on the old abbey gateway, Grange Walk.

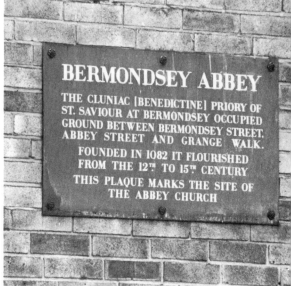

Above: The commemorative plaque on the wall of Chartes House, Abbey Street.

Opposite: The old charity school in Grange Walk. Before 1830 a girls school ran from a room over the porch at St Mary's.

GRANGE ROAD

Like Abbey Street, Grange Road may at a glance appear dull; but although it is a domestic street, with its pubs, cafes and shops, it contains some architectural surprises. The Education Department of the London Borough of Southwark has only to be contrasted with the old Bacon's School of 1890 on the corner and the Boutcher School of 1871 further down the road for us to realise how far away we are now from the Victorian age: a soulless, conformist, corporatist mentality completely at odds with the spirit of another age.

On the corner of Griggs Place is an old pub building dated 1898, and the adjacent terrace is dated 1896.

Grange Road is dominated by one of Southwark's tallest buildings. The Alaska business centre opposite the Spa Road junction was designed by Wallis Gilbert, and erected in 1932. It was occupied by Martin's fur factory until the 1970's. Renovated by Charterhouse Estates, the building was re-opened in 1991.

66, THE GRANGE.

GRANGE WALK

Grange Walk, by way of contrast, is, at its uppermost end, much quieter and more domestic. Indeed we feel almost like intruders into a very private place of residence, where we sense the continuing presence of history. Numbers 5-7 are of medieval origin and formed one side of the abbey gatehouse; numbers 8-11 are early eighteenth century, as is number 67; the old charity school is dated 1830, and the house adjacent to it is dated 1896, the terrace is 1890.

On the corner of Fendall Street the converted Grange Walk Infants School of 1853 and the 1980's Melford Court with its port-hole windows, and wrought iron stairways leading to first floor entrances all remind us that we are in a place of strictly private property.

After the Red Cow pub the walk changes its character drastically: council blocks loom on both sides of the road; Mabel Godwin House belongs to the Social Services Department of the Council, and close by the Larnaca Works building provides artists' studio space.

At the end of the walk we find a large building site: here Barrats are building homes for the South London Family Housing Association.

Above: A drawing, 1812, of the Grange farmhouse, which belonged to the Abbey, and provides the origin of the street names The Grange, Grange Road, and Grange Walk.

Above: Messrs. James Garnar's Leather manufactory, The Grange; an engraving from A Descriptive Account of Southwark & Bermondsey W.T. Pike, 1894.

GRANGE ROAD

ST. MARY MAGDALEN NATIONAL SCHOOLS, BERMONDSEY.

Above: An illustration from the Illustrated London News, 1872; now known as the Boutcher School commemorating its founder William Boutcher.

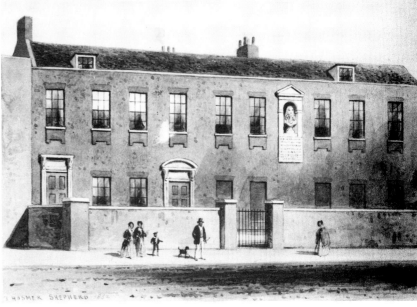

Above: A water-colour drawing by T.H. Shepherd, 1852, of the original Bacon's School built 1718. The later building of 1890 is shown on the cover of this publication. Courtesy: Trustees of the British Museum.

Opposite: The entrance way to the Alaska business complex. Two leather vats have been preserved and one in just noticeable in the courtyard.

LONG LANE AND ENVIRONS

Above: Two engravings of Long Walk, opposite Bermondsey Square, from the Builder, August 7th 1858.

Above: An engraving of St Paul's Church and school, architect S.S. Teulon, situated in Kipling Street; from the Illustrated London News, 1848.

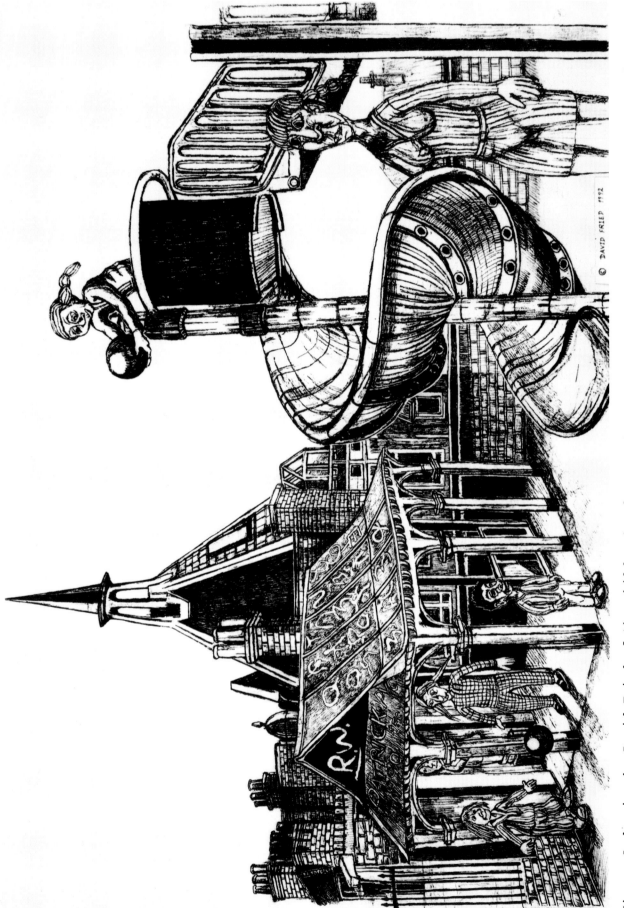

Above: A drawing by David Fried of the children's playground and shelter (demolished in 1992) at the end of Long Lane, overlooking Cluny Place, with the turret of the South London Mission in the background. A plaque records that the site was a quaker burial ground from 1697 until its closure in 1855. A few grave stones remain in one corner.

ABBEY STREET

Opposite: The memorial to Violet Alice Tritton, (died in 1957) on the wall of Bromleigh House, off Abbey Street. She was a much loved and respected worker at the Dockhead branch of the Time & Talents Association for many years. Dockhead House at 225, Abbey Street opened in 1931 and was demolished in 1957.

Above: A drawing from Bermondsey Walk, London Borough of Southwark, 1984. Courtesy: London Borough of Southwark.

Above: A drawing from The Doc by Barclay Baron, Edward Arno 1952. The building no longer stands.

Opposite: A drawing, 1835, of London to Greenwich Viaduct crossing Abbey Street.

Above: A drawing by David Fried of one of the foot tunnels, held up by cast iron columns, at the far end of Abbey Street.

ABBEY STREET

Abbey Street was laid out in 1820. Several old terraces remain. Dockhead House, part of the Time and Talents Association, and the Oxford Medical Mission (continuing today as the Oxford and Bermondsey Boys Club in Webb Street) have gone. Gone too is the Star Music Hall (which stood opposite the present day Neckinger Mills building); founded in 1867 it became a cinema in 1919 and since 1939 was a warehouse. Neckinger Mills with its tower draws the eye downwards beyond the railway bridge, and reminds us of the long association of the Bevington family with the area. Their tannery was established in 1802 on the site of a former paper mill, now occupied by the Neckinger estate. The firm moved out of the area about a decade ago. The Fleece pub on this corner of Neckinger Road brings visual interest to a street which today aches with boredom; but nearby comes a surprise: two foot tunnels under the railway line are held up by curious Greek doric cast iron columns: a setting for a bizarre encounter perhaps? David Fried thought so and he was thrilled by this subject when I first pointed it out.

BUTLERS WHARF

This is a place which is struggling hard to come to life again after redevelopment. Will it succeed? Will the vacant units soon fill with new businesses? Will this become a kind of new Covent Garden? It is hard to tell as everyone stares into the recessionary months, indeed years ahead.
 Art shows try to bring excitement into the empty units around Tower Bridge Piazza. Anthony Donaldson's Waterfall sculpture and Torso perched up high on a plinth in Brewery Square try to excite the vulgar curiosity of tourists. Other pieces of art can be found: Eduardo Paolozzi's cracked head sculpture outside the Design Museum, and the somewhat bemused, world weary donkey by Shirley Pace in the centre of Andrew Wadsworth's exclusive housing development known as the Circle.
 If most types of business have problems, then at least there is probably some chance for food and drink. In the Piazza we find the Bespoke Sandwich Company, and the brand new food shop Essentials And Lots More, where supermarket products lie beside designer packaged fancy items. In Shad Thames we find Le Pont de la Tour, wine merchants, restaurant, food store and bakery; and in Queen Elizabeth Street the Circle East restaurant; there is the Anchor Tap pub (the first pub to be owned by John Courage) in Horsleydown Lane, the Blue Print cafe in the Design Museum, and Jumbley's in Gainsford Street. Tea and coffee themselves are indeed celebrated in a brand new museum the Bramah Tea and Coffee Museum in the Clove Building in Maguire Street. Its hugue collection of teapots and its interesting pictures bring creativity and playfulness into our lives when weariness seems ever present. We wander down the long staircase grateful to Edward Bramah's enterprise for this unusual museum.

JACOB STREET

Opposite: Three Tuns Tavern, Jacob Street; a water-colour drawing by T.H. Shepherd, 1854 (from Crace Collection, British Museum). Courtesy: Trustees of the British Museum.

Below (left): A drawing by Sydney Jones (from his Thames Triumphant, 1943) of Eckett Street (now demolished) which ran between Jacob St and Wolseley St.

Above: Vogan's Mill, built 1989 for the Rosehaugh Co-partnership Development Ltd, this is a 15 storey block of flats, designed by Michael Squire Associates, replacing a white concrete silo on the site. Vogan's Mill was a complex of warehouses used since 1813 by the Vogan family for processing grain and cereal.

THE CIRCLE, QUEEN ELIZABETH STREET

The Circle complex of apartments at the far end of Queen Elizabeth Street with their bright purple walls was designed by Campbell, Zogolovitch, Wilkinson and Gough, 1990 for the Jacob Island Co. Plc Another, different view of the complex can be had from Tooley Street.

Opposite: Sculpture by Shirley Pace entitled 'Jacob, the Circle dray horse', to commemorate the brewery stables formerly on the site.

Above: Engraving of fire at the premises of Messrs. Barry Brothers, Meriton's Wharf, Dockhead, 1864.

Above: A lithograph (from the Crace Collection, British Museum) of St Saviour's Dock, early nineteenth century. Centuries ago this was a landing point for goods for the Abbey of St Saviour (Bermondsey Abbey), and the inlet point for the now vanished Neckinger river. Courtesy: Trustees of the British Museum.

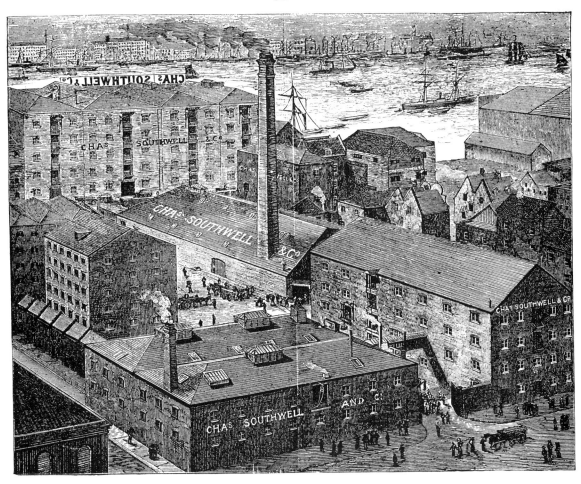

Above: Works of Messrs Charles Southwell & Co, Dockhead; wholesale and export manufacturers of jams, jellies, marmalade, candied peels, etc. The Dockhead works opened in 1885 and consisted of sixteen distinct buildings; a drawing from A Descriptive Account of Southwark and Bermondsey, W.T. Pike, 1894.

Opposite: This pub stands opposite St Saviour's Dock. This stretch of Jamaica Rd was formerly known as Dockhead.

BERMONDSEY WALL AND ENVIRONS

Above: A lithograph by Thomas Robert Way, from Reliques of Old London upon the banks of the Thames and in the suburbs south of the river, Bell, 1899, of the old manor house (now demolished), situated just south of Bermondsey Wall.

Above: An etching, 1934, by Nathaniel Kornbluth, of Bermondsey Wall. This riverside street runs southwards from the top of Mill Street to Cherry Garden Pier.

Above: An engraving from the Illustrated London News, 1849, of Christ Church and schools, situated in Parker's Row, just north of Abbey Street junction.

Above: Farncombe Street School, 1874 (now known as Riverside Primary School); Bevington Street facade.

Above: St Joseph's Catholic Primary School, 1912, George Row.

Above: No. 5, Bermondsey Wall (now demolished): a drawing by Hubert Williams.

AS SEEN BY "GAL."

The Hon. Member for West Bermondsey.

Above: A caricature from the Bermondsey Labour Magazine, November 1927.

DOCTOR SALTER

Opposite and below right: Dr Salter's day dream; a new work of sculpture by Diane Gorvin close to Cherry Garden Pier. A cat on the wall behind the child is also part of the sculpture. Dr Alfred Salter is an important personality in Bermondsey's development in the 1920's and '30's. He was a much loved doctor, Councillor and MP (from 1922). His pioneering re-building scheme is commemorated in the Alfred Salter Conservation Area to the South of Cherry Garden Pier.

Above: A drawing by W.G. Newton, 1910, from The Doctor, by Barclay Baron, Edward Arnold, 1952.

CAMBRIDGE UNIVERSITY MISSION AND BERMONDSEY SETTLEMENT

Above: A drawing from an annual report of the Cambridge University Mission, 1953/4. The Cambridge University Mission at 43, Old Jamaica Rd, dates back to 1906 when the Rev. H.D. Salmon, of Queen's College, Cambridge started a boys club and public dispensary at 47, Jamaica Rd. Today, it is still a flourishing organisation and the home mission of the Cambridge Inter-Collegiate Christian Union. It engages in youth work, through weekly clubs for young people, detached community work - meeting people where they are, gives encouragement, advice and support to families, and runs a resource centre for young unemployed adults.

Above: A drawing from The Leisure Hour, 1895.
The Bermondsey settlement opened in 1892 in Farncombe St. Dr Rev. John Scott Lidgett who founded it was warden from 1892 to 1949. Between 1909-1918 it was part of the South London Mission, rejoining 1954-1967. Scott Lidgett's long association with the area is remembered in a nearby Scott Lidgett Crescent. His bust can be found in the church at the South London Mission. The settlement closed and was demolished in 1969. A full account of its educational, religious and community work is to be found in John Beasley's The bitter cry heard and heeded.

Drawings from article in the Leisure Hour, 1895, part of its series on London settlements.

SOUTH BERMONDSEY

You can reach South Bermondsey by train from London Bridge; yet, its atmosphere is one of remoteness, and strangeness, a place way off the beaten track, a place which doesn't feel like London at all.

Forgotten, victorian churches stand stranded in alien landscapes of council housing: St Anne's in Thorburn Square, St Augustine's in Lynton Road, and St Bartholomew's in Barkworth Road.

The Upper Secondary Support Centre in Coopers Road, just off Rolls Road stands in bewildered isolation: a relic of the Victorian age dwarfed by threatening tower blocks at its rear.

Yet, people living here manage to have fun. When I was there, one Saturday afternoon a cavalcade of roller-skaters came pouring down Ilderton Road, on their way to a jamboree in Senegal Fields. Nearby in Eugenia Rd a big occasion was going on at St Katherine's Church. The street was crowded with black people in their religious finery, in flowing, long white robes and multi-coloured hats, little kids jumping about in a state of ecstatic excitement.

Opposite: St Anne's, Thorburn Square, built 1869-70, architect J. Porter.

Below: St Augustine's Church vicarage, a drawing by Martin Millard, 1992. St Augustine's is one of London's lesser known monumental churches. It was built 1875-1883, architects Henry Jarvis & Son (builders of many South London churches).

Above: Cliftonville Tavern, Verney Rd, at Ilderton Rd junction. The current pub sign shows a man in bathing suit being bitten by a crab, with white cliffs in the background.

Opposite: Christ Apostolic Chur[ch]
Ilderton Rd. Previously a bapti[st]
church, erected 1895, architect
George Baines.

Above: Upper Secondary Suppor[t]
Centre, Coopers Rd.

Opposite: St Bartholomew's
Church, Barkworth Rd, built
1866-7, architect E.
Taprell Allen

WEST LANE

Above: A portrait by Rose Cecil, 1980's, of 'Peter, the fruit and veg man'.
The artist writes:
"His shop is called George Staples and is on the corner of West Lane and
Jamaica Road. They must have been there for years and have alot of regular
customers. He was incredibly kind and patient with me, and I grew to be
very fond of him and his wife."

SOUTHWARK PARK

If you progress eastwards from Bermondsey you come to one of South London's largest open spaces: Southwark Park. This wide open space marks the boundary between Bermondsey and Rotherhithe: a place to get both places into perspective, a place from where you can go forwards or backwards in time.

Artists come down here to deposit and hang their works at the mysterious little Cafe Gallery tucked away beside the rose garden, run by Bermondsey Artists Group, shows come and go here throughout the year.

Children cart wheel, fly their kites, ride their bikes, endless games of football go on here, endless games of ball, the balls go to and fro, sports events in the stadium, jogging, sunbathing, couples making love. This is a park to which people come to be themselves.

The childrens' play rooms are decorated with two murals: one of tropical life, with baboons and flamingoes, and one of English country farm animals; no doubt all this is politically correct. In another children's play area, we encounter a group of gigantic play sculptures: a shoe, a gaping mouth, a severed hand - symbols perhaps for their creators, but no-one comes to Southwark Park to ponder on all the things that happen to people in life.

Surrey Quays shopping centre and the twinkling Canary Wharf tower on the horizon suggest that we are in a kind of fairy tale fantasy land, and we can go home from Southwark Park feeling less worried about everything.

On another occasion I came here again and strayed into the old English rose garden, initiated by Ada Salter and opened in autumn 1936. I noted:

A decadent sadness pervades this garden at the end of a long Saturday afternoon in July. Youths with earprings fish in the lake. A girl with holes in her tights walks around holding a rose. Is she lovesick? bored? an idiot? I don't know. A man sits motionless on a seat, then goes to the railing at the lake side, stares into the water, and then slowly walks away. A young aspiring writer sits scribbling with his beloved fountain pen and note book. No busts grace the stone columns, no fountains play; the broken down seats set out in a half circle around the rose bed are empty: the performance has long finished.

IN AND AROUND SOUTHWARK PARK

Above: Wood engraving by Peter Kennedy, used for the poster of the 1991 Bermondsey Artists Group summer show.

Above: Field Marshall Sir William Gomm, Constable of the Tower of London commemorated in a pub sign in Southwark Park Rd. The Gomms were Lords of the Manor of Rotherhithe in the nineteenth century. His wife is remembered in the former Lady Gomm Cottage Hospital, Hawkstone Rd, 1885 (above left), now part of LBS Social Services Department.

Above: Fountain memorial to Jabez West erected in Southwark Park in 1885; from 1838 he was much involved with temperance work in Bermondsey.

CENTRAL ROTHERHITHE AND ROTHERHITHE STREET

Rotherhithe village is a little bit of eighteenth and nineteenth century time all bottled up, a tiny corner of the metropolis which frequently features in guide books, where the church, charity school, Mayflower Inn, and the Brunel Engine House are all dutifully listed. This is a film set location - indeed reality and fiction can easily become entangled here. When I was there once a screeching police van disturbed the peace of early evening; a policeman and policewoman jumped out, they charged into a nearby housing estate, pounced on their suspect, bundled him into the van and slammed the door; yet, we have become so media blinkered, that I do not know whether this was truth or fiction.

Rotherhithe Street can be perambulated from top to bottom with interest. It offers surprises and stimulation for those attentive to the changing landscape. Most of the warehouses around the church date from the middle to the end of the nineteenth century: No 99, East India Wharf (c. 1850-60); No 101 (mid to late nineteenth century); No 105 (c. 1890-1900); Nos 111-115, Thames Tunnel Mills (mid nineteenth century); No 119 Grice's Wharf (c. 1850), linked by walkway to Grice's Granary (late eighteenth century); Nos 121-123, Tunnel Wharf; Nos 137-131, Brandram's Wharf (c. 1870-80). No 135 is a mid nineteenth century barge building and repair works (Charles Hay & Son, established in 1789).

A place full of sombre old warehouses, done up and inhabited by yuppies, trendies and the nouveaux riches of the 1980's, a cynical observer may say. Yet, if one continues just a bit further down the road the landscape changes. Adjacent to Charles Hay's is a newly landscaped riverside area Cumberland Wharf (opposite Swan Rd), considerably enhanced by a recently created sculpture, Peter MacLean's Sunbeam Weekly and the Pilgrim's Pocket. It is worth a close inspection: sculpted into the pages of the comic one discovers an array of images: all kinds of things which have come to us from the New World by way of exchange. A Staffordshire bull terrier on its hind legs brings us back to present day reality.

A little further on one encounters the red painted, iron bascule bridge which Don Jarvis thought worth recording in a drawing. It leads us into the Surrey Water housing area, where the expanse of water, the fountain, the landscaping, and low rise housing all create a soothing atmosphere of tranquility. Is this some kind of rural, urban dreamland, one may wonder, where all the problems of life disappear as if by magic? No doubt the property developers have marketed this site and others in Surrey Docks as such; and a further escape root is at hand. A long road Dock Hill Avenue leads us to a new artificial mound Stave Hill, created by L.D.D.C. in 1985, with the ecological park to the north (established by the Trust for Urban Ecology in 1987), and Russia Dock woodland to the south. Stave Hill offers impressive panoramic views, a place to pause on, and to get our bearings, and also an opportunity to see another piece of work by Michael Rizello (sculptor of the bust of engineer James Walker at Brunswick Quay): his relief model of the Surrey Docks complex reminds us that L.D.D.C. has not forgotten the past.

But, to return to Rotherhithe Street: a little further on at Island Yard we find, perhaps surprisingly, a brand new youth hostel: a building which is pleasing to look at, a building for people, not a cardboard cut out... Globe Wharf warehouse of 1883 is currently awaiting redevelopment, while across the road Amos Estate, once notorious for its decay, has now been renovated and refurbished. When it was very run down Gavin Parry photographed the strange inhabitants of this estate, and showed his prints at a photographic exhibition at the Cafe Gallery, in Southwark Park in 1987. Where are these people today? Another building awaiting new uses is the old fire station, built in 1902. Standing in isolation, this is how a building looks when it has come to the very end of its previous history. Opposite lies the Lavender Pond Nature Park, and the old pumping station which now houses the recently opened Rotherhithe Heritage Museum.

As Rotherhithe Street bends round, we come to another major redevelopment site centring around the old Nelson Dock: the former steam engine house, of about 1900, now a museum, and Nelson House, 1740 (both previously premises of Mills & Knight), a new conference centre, the Scandic Crown Hotel, and new housing at Lawrence Wharf all transform a site with an historic ship-building and repair tradition. Further new developments continue: the Trinity Business Centre, and the Surrey Docks Farm.

At the bottom end of Rotherhithe Street one encounters the Docklands Settlement with its chapel of 1871, still surviving as a community organisation.

A CEREMONY AT BARNARD'S WHARF

"You are invited to the ceremony on Friday at 11.30 am" Philip Bews the sculptor from Runcorn told me on the telephone late one evening. Barnard's Wharf is a newly landscaped riverside walk adjacent to Surrey Docks farm, initiated by former L.D.D.C. landscape architect Fraser Bordwick, it is enlivened with a procession of sculpted animals: a fox and dog (by Marjan Wouda), two goats and two kids (by Althea Wynne), barn owl and mouse (by Nathan David), three geese and a cat (by Diane Gorvin), a donkey, two pigs and two piglets (by Philip Bews). A little ceremony had been arranged to celebrate these newly made pieces. It was a strange occasion: I found the place at last. There were little groups of people of various ages and backgrounds standing around. I felt almost like an intruder, attending a function which was not intended for me. I found two of the artists: Philip Bews and Diane Gorvin, with their parents and friends from the North-West, looking slightly bemused by their surroundings. Top brass people from the L.D.D.C. were there too. People from the local housing estate were there: brand new people in brand new houses; somebody wanted to complain about the railings. Vivaldi came out of the loudspeaker. We were summoned to the official opening: an actor from Emmerdale Farm had come to unveil a plaque. And then we all lined up for dinner in a marquee. Two people behind me spoke worriedly about the problems of finding work, of how to make money. Eventually I was fed, I took my plate and glass and sat looking at the Isle of Dogs.

Above: A coloured etching by Peter Chase, 1986, showing vista of Rotherhithe Street from the Wapping riverside; a view much favoured by artists, Peter Chase has imbued his vision with a haunting nostalgia.

Above: A drawing by Geoffrey Appleton depicting Rotherhithe life and buildings, first published in By peaceful means: the story of Time and Talents 1887-1987 by Marjorie Daunt. In front of St Mary's church stands the old Mortuary which was reopened in 1980 as the new base for the organisation.

Above: An etching of the view of Rotherhithe riverside from Cherry Garden Pier, by Nathaniel Kornbluth, 1934. Characteristically his figures have their backs turned, and seem engaged in somewhat dubious activity.

CHURCHES: OLD AND NEW

Above: St Crispin's, Southwark Park Rd, designed by T.F. Ford, 1958-9, replacing an earlier church of 1879-80.

Above: World War I memorial in Trinity Church churchyard.

Opposite: The old Trinity Church, Rotherhithe Street, architect S. Kempthorne; bombed and replaced by a new church, 1959, architect T.F. Ford.

Below: St Katharine's, Eugenia Rd, architect W.O. Milne, built 1884, replaced by a new church in 1960, architects Covell, Matthews.

TRINITY CHURCH, ROTHERHITHE,
Consecrated 1838.

TRINITY CHURCH SCHOOLS, *Erected* 1836.

Above: This building still stands close to the new Trinity Church, and is used for community and business functions.

ST HELENA GARDENS

Above: St Helena Tavern, St Helena Gardens, Rotherhithe; a water-colour drawing by J.T. Wilson, 1870. Courtesy: South London Art Gallery. The gardens opened in 1770 and were popular for their concerts, dancing and other entertainments. Unlike Bermondsey Spa the gardens appear to have survived for many decades until about 1881. St Katharine's Church in Eugenia Road, south of St Helena Rd, stands on part of the site.

ROTHERHITHE TUNNEL

Above: Rotherhithe entrance to the tunnel; an illustration from the London Illustrated News, 1843.

The building of the tunnel was an immensely protracted operation: construction work commenced in 1825; work ceased between 1828 and 1835 due to lack of finance, and the tunnel finally opened in 1843 with government financial assistance. It was converted into the underground railway line in 1865-9.

Opposite: Rotherhithe underground, a drawing by Don Jarvis (from his Souvenir of Rotherhithe No 2)

ROTHERHITHE STREET AND ENVIRONS

18th century houses in Rotherhithe Street before demolition: a drawing by Dennis Flanders published in the Illustrated London News, 1962. The Jolly Waterman pub stood next to Queen's House. Queen's House was run originally as a mission by Queen's College, Cambridge, and later 1941-53 as a community centre by the Time and

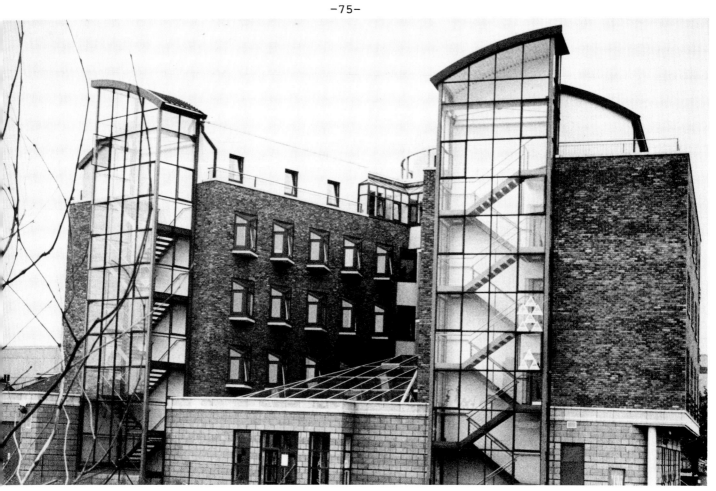

Above: The new youth hostel at Island Yard, Salter Rd. Built 1991, architects Alan Turner Associates. Also offers conference and meeting facilities and a self service restaurant open to the local community.

Opposite: Docklands Settlement, with chapel building, at far end of Rotherhithe Street; opened in 1871 as a Norwegian Seaman's Mission.

Opposite: Lavender Dock Pumping Station, now housing the Rotherhithe Heritage Museum, built 1930 to regulate water levels in Surrey Docks. Also shown is the new nature park.

Opposite: An unusually dra[wn]
wall on warehouse East Ind[ia]
Wharf, at top of Rotherhit[he]
Street, with riverside sea[t]

Opposite: A drawing by Martin
Millard, 1992 of the disused
London Hydraulic Pumping Power
Company pumping station in
Renforth Street. Built in 1902 a[nd]
operational until 1977.

Above: A drawing by Don Jarvis, 1979, from his Souvenir of Rotherhithe No 2 showing the back of the Mayflower pub in Rotherhithe Street. The pub, originally known as the Shippe was built about 1550; rebuilt in the eighteenth century, and renamed The Spread Eagle and Crown; renamed again about twenty years ago. Captain Christopher Jones sailed in his Mayflower for America from here, returning in 1621. He is buried in St Mary's churchyard.

Above: 'Sunbeam Weekly and the Pilgrim's Pocket', a bronze sculpture by Peter McLean, at Cumberland Wharf (opposite Swan Rd)

Above: Memorial in St Mary's Churchyard to Edward Blick, Rector of the church 1835-67. He was especially active in establishing other churches and schools in the area.

Above: A pump built in 1929, used at Lavender Dock Impounding Station until 1969. Now located outside the Brunel Engine House.

Above: Stone from Surrey Docks, in Kings Stairs Gardens (close to the Angel pub), unveiled by the Queen on her jubilee visit in 1977.

Above: A drawing by Don Jarvis, 1979, from his Souvenir of Rotherhithe No 2, of the iron bascule bridge, Rotherhithe Street over entrance canal to area now known as Surrey Water (formerly basin of Albion Dock).

Above: Shipbuilder's Yard, Rotherhithe Street; watercolour drawing by James Lawson Stewart, 1880's. Courtesy: South London Art Gallery.

Above: A drawing by Sydney Jones
of Nelson Dry Dock, and old Georgian
house from The Sphere.

Nelson Dry Dock was built about 1790. At its head is the former steam engine house of about 1900, shown below, now a small museum and interpretation centre.
Behind Nelson House (built 1740), can be seen the twin seven storey block of the new hotel on either side of the old Nelson Dock, which dates back to the mid 17th century.

ALBION STREET

If the topmost end of Rotherhithe Street is a little bit of bottled up history, Albion Street is perhaps a corner of present day sad little England. Here, indeed, is a pub called The Little Crown. It stands opposite the Finnish Seaman's Mission, of 1959. Its bell tower looks as if inspired by the tower of a fire station. Its starkness confronts the charm of St Mary's church spire across the road.

On one side of the road is the Rotherhithe Civic Centre. The statue Bermondsey Boy, by Tommy Steele, erected in 1975 in front of the centre has vanished. Who took it away? On the other side is a string of shops: betting shop, grocer, hairdresser, cleaners, butcher, chemist, food take aways, an Indian restaurant. At one end of the street is the Albion pub, at the other end the Lord Nelson.

But here in Albion Street, as in Brunel Road and Renforth Street we are jerked out of inertia and sadness into a state of disturbance. Scrawled on the wall is a noisy reminder that a local youth has been killed, followed by a police cover up. What is happening in Rotherhithe village?

RENFORTH STREET

A turning called Renforth Street, leading off Albion Street, takes us to one of Rotherhithe's less well-known monuments: the disused pumping station of 1902, owned by the London Hydraulic Power Company and operational until 1977. A sign tells us that it has been acquired for development by Jacobs Island Company. The chimney soars upwards; sparrows build nests in the crevices; pigeons squat on the railings above the metal panels; butterflies flit about. This is a building at the end of its history; protected by barbed wire, ugly grafitti is sprawled on the gates and walls.

Little kids ride about on their bikes; adults stray home from work, weary, bored, uncertain of their futures. A smart van parked nearby belongs to Melki, computer supplies specialists. Scaffolding stands around the base of the two council tower blocks. This is England, summer, 1992.

GREENLAND DOCK AND SURREY QUAYS AREA

This is a chunk of docklands which offers interest and stimulation for anyone seeking to fill an empty afternoon. The brand new shopping centre contains the predictable High Street chain stores, but it is bright and customer friendly, nautically inspired, and achieves a remarkable transformation of the area, when one remembers that this is the site of Canada Dock, warehouses and granaries. The two stunning murals at the entrance remind us where we actually are and the L.D.D.C. has placed one of its historical interpretation panels in the forecourt with a photograph of the once bustling dock.

Here at Surrey Quays one can enjoy wide open spaces; perhaps unlike anywhere else in central London one feels less hemmed in, less imprisoned. To the north there are unusual vistas: a landscape of church towers, the domes of Wolfe Crescent, the chimney of the disused pumping station, and low rise housing, some completed and occupied, some going up.

To the south lies the hugue expanse of Greenland Dock, now very quiet and silent. At dusk the swans and ducks cry out with muted anguish. They feel estranged and frightened by all the stillness around them. In the evening lights come on everywhere: they hang like poisonous oranges.

But, there are things to look at: the L.D.D.C. has done a careful job in landscaping and historical interpretation; everything of interest is labelled and explained: swing bridges, the local keepers office, the tide gauge house, hydraulic capstans, lock machinery. There are four large housing complexes: at Brunswick and Greenland Quays, at Swedish Quays, and at Greenland Passage on either side of the lock entrance to the dock.

I sat there one hot July afternoon; feeling bemused with the heat and unsure of what was going to become of me; people sprawled in the sunshine, fished, rode slowly about on their bikes; boys plunged in and out of the water, fooled around; gradually people in work strayed home... the planners and architects have all striven to produce an environment where people might enjoy living: shops, offices, a water sports centre, a marina, and a multitude of trees all show some sensitivity to people's actual needs. Yet, disaster looms... an article in the Southwark & Bermondsey News, July 30th, 1992 reports the closure of the marina, as the property firm Marinup PLC goes into liquidation. The future of Baltic Quay and Tavern Quay is also currently uncertain.

LOWER ROAD

This is an unusual thoroughfare with its strange variety of buildings: churches, pubs, shops, homes. At its topmost end, buildings of the powers that be: the Rotherhithe Evangelical Church, St Olave's Hospital, a council leisure centre (with its vivid yellow and blue semi-abstract mural), and the disused building of the local Labour Party. They mingle with smaller places: the Helen Pele almshouses, 1901, the Prince of Orange and the China Hall pubs, and the Swedish seaman's church.

The road changes its character at Surrey Quays underground station: a strange assortment of shops and businesses, some thriving, some struggling on both sides of the road: an estate agents, a driving school, Yum Yum pastries and sandwiches, Jays Jeans, Raceways motor-cycles, Muttleys pet foods, Dave's Cave (clothes and videos). Then come more pubs: the Farriers Arms, the Dreadnought, and at the end of Stanley Terrace (of about 1830) the Merry Cricketers. Close by is a branch of McDougals Restaurant: we are now in Evelyn Road, in another locality and another London Borough.

Above: Mural in entrance to Surrey Quays Shopping Centre. This dramatic composition, executed by the Murals and Banners partnership celebrates and records Surrey Docks' importance as a centre for the wood and grain trades.

Above: Former dock offices, built 1892, Surrey Quays Road.

Above: Deal porters sculpture, by Philip Bews (based on a photograph in an old training manual), Canada Water, Surrey Quays.

Above: A drawing by Martin Millard 1991 of the Baltic Quay complex at the head of South Dock, built 1990, architects Lister, Drew, Haines. It will house shops, offices and flats. The 14 storey tower, blue glass, yellow frames bring perhaps a jarring, almost discordant note to the sobriety of the other adjacent developments.

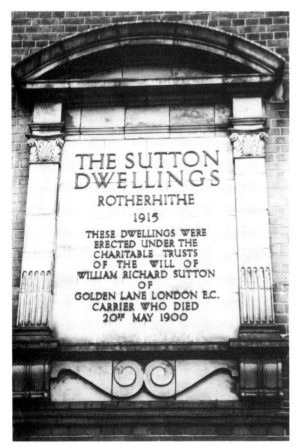

Above: Sutton Dwellings is a quiet, dignified estate off Plough Way. It makes a telling contrast with the post-modernist architecture around Greenland Dock.

Below: A drawing by Paul Middleton of new housing, 1990, architects Price, Cullen at Swedish Quays.

Above: 'Privileged ice': unloading ice for the hospitals only, despite the General Strike at the Surrey Commercial Docks. A drawing by H.W. Koekkoek, from the Illustrated London News, August 12th 1911.

Above: Bust sculpted by Michael Rizzello at Brunswick Quay, north east corner of Greenland Dock.

Above: Newly commissioned sculpture 'Curlicue' by William Pye, standing at Greenland Passage.

Above: The old Tide Gauge House.

Above: Hydraulic capstan, Greenland Dock; turned by high pressure water it helped ships in and out of the dock.

Above: Mural in entrance to Surrey Quays shopping centre, executed by Murals and Banners.

Above: L.C.C. flat, Redriff Estate, Rotherhithe: a wood engraving by Rachel Reckitt (published in London south of the river, by Sam Price Myers, Paul Elek, 1949).

Above: Rotherhithe Town Hall, Lower Road (subsequently Rotherhithe Library), architects Murray and Foster; a drawing from Building News, 20th September 1895. Destroyed by bombing, a new library was opened in 1975 as part of the new Rotherhithe Civic Centre in Albion Street.

Above: A drawing by David Fried of one of the Greek 'caryatids' (there is another on the other side of the wall) from the old Rotherhithe Public Library, sculpted by Henry Poole in 1897. This strange relic is located, somewhat off course and probably completely ignored, in a council estate just behind the Crossways United Reformed Church in New Kent Rd.

LOWER ROAD

Above: The Terris Theatre (also known as Rotherhithe Hippodrome), a drawing from the London Argus, 1899. It stood just north of the Town Hall/library, and was opened in 1899 by Ellaline Terriss, a well-known actress of the day; it was demolished in 1955.

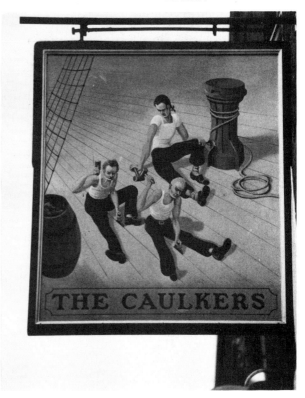

Below: An interesting pub sign, close to Surrey Quays tube station. A pub has stood here since the nineteenth century. Previously known as the Jolly Caulkers, it once had a sign painted by Cosmo Clark showing three less individualistic, but more industrious workers.

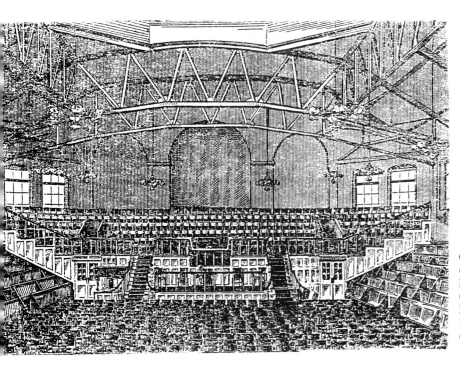

Opposite: Rotherhithe Great Hall, opened in 1906, the second building of the Rotherhithe Free Church. It was bombed and a new building Rotherhithe Evangelical Free Church was erected in the early 1960's.

Above: Rotherhithe Public Baths and Washhouses, architects George Elkington & Son, from the Builder, 19th February, 1881. Situated on the corner of Gomm Rd and Lower Rd (now site of Seven Islands Leisure Centre).

Above: All Saints' Church, Lower Rd (now demolished), an engraving by William Spence, 1840.

BIBLIOGRAPHY OF BOOKS AND ARTICLES ON BERMONDSEY AND ROTHERHITHE FOR FURTHER READING

The Autobiography of a Bermondsey boy, by F.B. 5 part series which was published in the 1924 issues of The Bermondsey Book (a quarterly review of life and literature).

BANBURY, Philip. Shipbuilders of the Thames and Medway. David and Charles, 1971.

BARON, Barclay. The doctor. Edward Arnold, 1952. An account of the work and life of Dr John Stansfield, founder of the Oxford Medical Mission of Bermondsey.

BARTLETT, Alan. The churches of Bermondsey, 1850-1914. Unpublished thesis 1981. (Copy in Southwark Local Studies Library).

BEASLEY, John D. The bitter cry heard and heeded: the story of the South London Mission of the Methodist Church, 1889-1989. South London Mission, 1989.

BECK, Edward Josselyn. Memorials to serve a history of the Parish of St Mary, Rotherhithe. Cambridge U.P., 1907.
Chapters on ecclesiastical records, old Rotherhithe families, physical aspects of Rotherhithe in 1800 (from notes of an old inhabitants recollections), the manor, Prince Lee Boo, docks, present day Christian organisations.

BERMONDSEY BOROUGH COUNCIL. Catalogue of prints and drawings in the Bermondsey Public Libraries, 1927. A useful source of information on work by prolific topographical artists such as J.C. Buckler, J.P. Emslie, R.J. Angel, with historical notes.

BERMONDSEY BOROUGH COUNCIL. The official guide. 8 editions published by Ed. J. Burrow, 1922-1951.
Editions for 1958, 1960 and 1963 published by the Pyramid Press.

BLICK, Edward. A short account of the churches, schools, and charities in the parish of St Mary, Rotherhithe, Seeley, 1848.

BOAST, Mary. The story of Bermondsey (Neighbourhood Histories Series No 5). Rev. edition. London Borough of Southwark, 1984. (Illustrations by Yvonne Hale). Gives references to published historical accounts of specific institutions.

BOAST, Mary. The story of Rotherhithe (Neighbourhood Histories Series No 6). London Borough of Southwark, 1980. (Illustrations by David Burch).

BROCKWAY, Fenner. Bermondsey story: the life of Alfred Salter. Allen & Unwin, 1949.

CHERRY, B. and PEVSNER, N. The Buildings of England: London, volume 2. Penguin, 1983. Gives a thorough survey of churches and other institutional buildings.

CLARKE, E.T. Bermondsey: its historic memories and associations. Elliot Stock, 1901. Illustrations include old and contemporary engravings. Chapters on the abbey, Bermondsey House, historical development and contemporary Bermondsey.

DAUNT, Marjorie. By peaceful means: the story of Time and Talents, 1887-1987. Time & Talents Association, 1989.

A Descriptive account of Southwark and Bermondsey, illustrated. W.T. Pike, 1894. Especially useful for its accounts of local firms.

LONDON DOCKLANDS DEVELOPMENT CORPORATION. Surrey Docks. (Heritage Walks Series). (Illustrations by Chris Marshall).

PHILLIPS, G.W. The history and antiquities of the Parish of Bermondsey. J. Unwin, 1841.

PIERS, Peregrine. Caledonian Market. Illustrated article on Bermondsey antiques market, in Bandwagon, October 1952.

PROCKTER, Adrian, editor. L & GR 150th anniversary, 1836-1986: London and Greenwich railway. London Reference Books, 1986.

SEWELL, Dorca. Life within the black square mile. 3 page article on the Bermondsey 'spirit', in the December, 1923 issue of the Bermondsey Book.

SOUTHWARK & BERMONDSEY NEWS. The following is a selection of informative articles which have appeared over the last few years:
December 6th, 1990: Harry Bowling: Bermondsey's own novelist.
May 9th, 1991: Ten years of the LDDC 1981-1991.
August 1st, 1991: Southwark & Bermondsey News: one hundred issues on. (5 page, illustrated article, highlighting some of the stories published October 1987-July 1991).
August 29th, 1991: Black and white in Bermondsey. (4 page, illustrated article on attitudes to racism).
October 10th, 1991: The award winning Surrey Docks. Details of 14 Bermondsey and Rotherhithe developments which have won awards.
October 10th, 1991: A day in the life of Tower Bridge Magistrate's Court.
October 24th, 1991: Shad Thames and Butler's Wharf: the buildings are beautiful, but where are the people? (Two page, illustrated article on businesses, housing and local people).
November 21st, 1991: An interview with Bob Mellish (MP for Bermondsey 1950-1983).
January 2nd, 1992: 1991: a year in the news. (Month by month survey of stories reported).
February 13th, 1992: Bermondsey's antiques market: the greatest market in the world.
May 21st, 1992: Fifteen years of Father Nick. (Nick Richards, St Mary's, Rotherhithe.
August 27th, 1992: Bermondsey from the river. (Series of 24 small photographs showing the changing landscape from Greenland Dock to London Bridge).

THE SOUTHWARK ANNUAL. Printed and published by Frederick Shaw & Co (Dockhead), 1893-1906.

STATHAM, James. The location and development of London's leather manufacturing industry since the early nineteenth century. London University thesis, 1965. (copy in Southwark Local Studies Library).

THOMAS, R.H.G. London's first railway: The London and Greenwich. Batsford, 1986.

WILKINSON, Tony. Down and out. Quartet, 1981. Includes accounts of Tower Bridge Hotel, and Tooley Hotel, two hostels for down and outs.

WILLIAMS, Stephanie. Docklands. Architecture Design and Technology Press, 1990. (ADT Architecture Guide Series). Illustrated, technical, critical appraisal of docklands architecture, new and old.

NOTES ON ARTISTS AND SCULPTORS FEATURED

ANGEL, R.J. Engineer and surveyor to the old Bermondsey Borough Council. His pen and ink drawings made during the first two decades of the century record many now vanished buildings. His work is held by Southwark Local Studies Library and has been reproduced in the B.B.C.'s official guides, its catalogue of prints and drawings, and Beck's History of Rotherhithe.

APPLETON, Geoffrey. Professional graphic artist, currently living in Greenwich.

BERMONDSEY ARTISTS GROUP. This 40 strong group of artists working in a variety of media and styles was formed in 1983, initially as the basis for a group show at London Bridge. It runs the Cafe Gallery in Southwark Park and stages an annual show of members work here. At the 1992 show only the work displayed by Harry Harmer related to the locality (three small oil paintings entitled: 'Blue Anchor', 'Underneath the arch, Bermondsey', and 'Old Shop, Bermondsey'.) Its members are active in schools through the Southwark Children's Foundation Artist in Residence Scheme and were involved with the murals displayed around the excavated site of Edward III's manor house (mid fourteenth century) in Cathay Street.
For the record the members of the group in 1992 were: David Allen, Bridget Anderson, Richard Atherton, Jane Barnes, Kevin Bolger, Joanna Braithwaite, Alistair Brotchie, Frances Coleman, Jane Colling, Richard Daniel, Jane Deakin, Steve Dunn, Jane Eyton, Judy Feasey, (her work includes some water-colour drawings of Rotherhithe village subjects). Tony Fleming, Adrian Ford, Clive Garland, Paul Green, Douglas Hall, Harry Harmer, Rita Harris, Ron Henocq, David John, Malcolm Jones, Colin Kennedy, Isis Matreya, Peter McLean, Gavin Parry, Narinda Singh Plahy, Vanessa Pooley, Emma Posey, Martin Pover, Roger Riley, Nicole Robinson, Alex Crombie-Rodgers, Pip Seymour, Louise Sheridan, Peter Stanyer, Jo Stockham, J. Tirimani, Nigel Tucker, Claire Waterhouse, Jessica Wilkes, Richard Wilson, Tim Wright and Ayten Zeki.
In 1987 the group staged an exhibition of Bermondsey and Rotherhithe photographs at the Cafe Gallery. This included work by David Allen, Frances Coleman, Jean Pierre Rodella, Adrian Ford, Harry Diamond, Ron Henocq, Gavin Parry, Vince Bevan, Edgardo Braggio, and Liz Light. Most recently the group has executed a mosaic mural of a swan and modern riverside developments at the Swan Estate, Rotherhithe.

BEWS, Philip. (b. 1951). He has always lived and worked in North West England. He trained and worked in the 1970's and early 1980's as a landscape architect, (with Runcorn New Town Development Corporation); since then he has studied and practised fine art and sculpture, working on a variety of projects. Between 1986 and 1988 he was sculptor in residence at Birchwood Community High School, working with local adults and school pupils to make sculpture in a wide range of materials. His Deal Porters was commissioned by L.D.D.C. as were his pig, piglets and donkey, part of the collection of farm animals in cast bronze at Barnard's Wharf, adjacent to Surrey Docks Farm. He has published an illustrated booklet on his Birchwood residency.

CECIL, Rose. Lady Cecil is a member of the great English family the Cecils of Hatfield House. She was living at Corbetts Wharf, Bermondsey Wall East in the mid 1980's and made a range of pictures of dockland subjects, including demolition scenes. Her Victoria Royal Dock oil painting is reproduced in <u>A London Docklands Album</u> (Peter Marcan Publications, 1992). She is a naturally talented artist who can create appealing and unusual pictures from any subject matter that attracts her. Her portraits are especially sensitive.

CHASE, Peter. Print-maker and teacher at Bournemouth College of Art. At the instigation of East End art dealer Andrew Lamont he made a series of atmospheric, haunted coloured etchings of riverside and dockland subjects in the mid 1980's, including 'Evening Light, Rotherhithe'. More recently he has depicted Blackfriars, Albert and Chelsea Bridges, Battersea Power Station, and St Paul's Cathedral.

FLANDERS, Dennis. (b. 1915). Well-known, prolific topographical and architectural artist, working in black and white, and watercolour. He was a 'special' artist on the Illustrated London News from 1956 to 1964. His books include a major collection of some 224 drawings, <u>Britannia</u>: being a selection from the work of Dennis Flanders...landscape and architecture of the British Isles, Oriel Press, 1984.

FRIED, David George. His pen and ink drawings reproduced in this publication were especially commissioned. His biographical details are given in <u>An East London Album</u> (Peter Marcan Publications, 1992), which reproduces two of his works. He is particularly sensitive to the decadence of inner city life, and his drawings of small, bewildered figures dwarfed by strange relics from the past make a telling comment on our society which often seems close to the end of its history. He is also a gifted book illustrator: <u>Angst und Trost</u> (stories of Jews and Nazis by Erich Fried), Alibaba (Frankfurt), 1983; <u>Comrades for the Charter</u>, by Geoffrey Trease, Alibaba, 1984; <u>The red towers of Granada</u>, by Geoffrey Trease, Alibaba, 1984; <u>Kalender fur den Frieden</u> (Peace Calender), Bund Verlag, Cologne, 1985; <u>Bedenkliche Zeiten</u> (anthology about Hiroshima and Nagasaki), Bund Verlag, 1985.

GABAIN, Ethel. (1883-1950). Distinguished, but little known lithographer, the wife of the very original print-maker John Copley. Most of her 300 odd lithographs up to the early 1930's are of adolescent and young women in intimate interior settings, as well as a series on the French pantomime character Pierrot. Her prints executed as an Official War artist in the 1940's form a vivid and technically accomplished record of war time work and activity. The Ministry of Information published two sets of her lithographs: Children in wartime; and Women's Work in the war. Catalogue number 34, 1985, from the print dealers Garton and Cooke is a useful survey of the two artists' output.

GORVIN, Diane. Partner of Philip Bews (see above), she was employed as a sculptor by Warrington & Runcorn Development Corporation 1982-86. Her work there is described and illustrated in their booklet <u>Sculpture in the new town</u>. Since 1978 she has carried out a wide variety of public commissions, and most recently executed the three geese and cat at Barnard's Wharf, adjacent to Surrey Docks Farm. Her most striking work to date may well be her three piece Doctor Salter's Daydream, with its interesting use of the wall and seating at the newly landscaped riverside walk close to Cherry Garden Pier.

HASSELDINE, Ernest. Illustrator associated with the South London Mission, his drawings appear in their annual reports of the early 1920's, in Walter Spencer's account of the mission <u>The glory in the garret</u>, published in 1932 by the Epworth Press, and in <u>Ballads of Bermondsey</u>, by Leslie Davison, published in 1943 also by the Epworth Press.

JANES, Norman Thomas (1892-1980). Landscape artist, working in waercolour, etching, and wood engraving, he taught at Hornsey School of Art, 1928-60, and the Slade 1936-50. He was attracted to coastal, and riverside subject matter, often with boats, and two further examples of his work are reproduced in <u>Artists and the East End</u> (Peter Marcan Publications, 1986).

JARVIS, Don. Ever since studying painting at Camberwell School of Art in the 1950's, he has been especially interested in London riverside subject matter. He was active in Rotherhithe from about 1975-1985, producing many drawings and paintings of the locality. Drawings were published as two booklets: <u>Souvenir of Rotherhithe</u>, Nos 1 and 2, in 1979. His Aard Press has also issued a booklet/A3 broadsheet on Tower Bridge, a collection of poems and drawings <u>Riverline</u> (riverside from Wandsworth to Woolwich), post-card reproductions of drawings, poetry, artists bookworks, mailart documentation and badges.

JONES, Syndey Robert. 1981-1966. Noteworthy for his carefully observed, detailed topographical work in many books published by The Studio, including <u>London Triumphant</u>, 1942, and <u>Thames Triumphant</u>, 1943. He also contributed to the Sphere.

KEMP, David. (b. 1945). David Kemp has lived in West Cornwall since 1972. He was born in the East End of London. He spent four years at sea in the Merchant Navy before art school. He has been making outdoor public sculpture since 1981 and his extraordinary assemblages using materials ranging from bronze and welded steel to masonry and heavy timber have captivated and delighted the public: witty, yet disturbing comments on the industrial and technological culture of the nineteenth and twentieth centuries. His most recent piece 'Vox populaire' has been installed in the reception of the advertising agency Ogilvy and Mather at Cabot Square, Canary Wharf. Other public pieces include: 'Heavy Plant' 20 feet high, a centrepiece at the new Sheffield Science Park; the 30 foot long 'Iron Horse' commissioned by Tyne and Wear PTC for their Four Lane Ends Metro Station; and 'The Old Transformers', two Easter Island style heads overlooking the site of the former Consett Steelworks.

KENNEDY, Colin. Printmaker and member of the Bermondsey Artists Group, currently living in Brighton. His coloured print 'Picnic in Southwark Park' depicts a figure in a balloon labelled B.A.G. snatching up a picnicker and his dog. It was used as the invitation card for the 1992 show.

KORNBLUTH, Nathaniel. The artist's atmospheric, yet topographically precise etchings and drawings of vanished London: buildings, canal, dock and riverside scenes have enjoyed a great revival of interest in the 1980's since executed in the early 1930's. His work has been exhibited by and taken up by the Lamont Gallery in Bethnal Green, and also features in Artists and the East End (Peter Marcan Publications, 1986), and A London Docklands Album (Peter Marcan Publications, 1992). He received instruction from Norman Janes, and it is interesting to contrast the two men's visions of the same subject: Cherry Garden Pier and adjacent warehouses.

McDONALD, Lesley. Born in Luton, raised and educated in Surrey. Now married with two children, she still finds time to take as many and as varied photographs as possible. She is currently studying to become a teacher of photography.

McLEAN, Peter. Educated at Cheethams music school, Manchester and Reading University, he has been living and working in Rotherhithe/Bermondsey for some 18 years, and was a founder member of the Bermondsey Artists Group. A year's residency at Redriff School recently culminated in the creation in 1990 of a Tug-boat sculpture standing at the entrance to the school. He works mainly in three quarter relief, normally in wood and glass. A recent project is Ten Deaths, humorous, fabled deaths of animals and people from myth and history.

MILLARD, Martin. Freelance artist and illustrator, with a special interest in black and white London topographical work. He is especially attracted to buildings at the end of their histories, and has drawn extensively in South London and the East End. He has a degree in Fine Art from the School of Visual Art, New York City. He is currently chairman of the Nine Elms Group of Artists (artists from Clapham, Vauxhall and Battersea), which holds annual exhibitions at the Painters Hall in the City. His drawings reproduced in this publication were especially commissioned.

MILNE, Vincent. The artist, who currently has a studio at Chisenhale Road Studios, was working in the late 1970's at Butlers Wharf and made a series of drawings of this locality. His Bermondsey Street mural made with Lynette Lombard in 1981 has sadly deteriorated, but when first painted it made an extremely bright and attractive display of scenes from Bermondsey's past and present (monastery, wine vaults, printing, docks, tanning and leather trade, the first public laundry, the celebration for the Queen's 1977 Jubilee at Brunswick Court, bonfire night, hop-picking, the antiques trade).

MURALS AND BANNERS. The two artists behind this enterprise are Carol Kenna and Stephen Lobb. They are based at Greenwich Mural Workshop, MacBean Centre, Macbean St, Woolwich, London SE18 and work with a wide variety of clients. They produce guides and handbooks, and carry out consultancy and educational work. The 'Wind of Peace' mural in Creek Rd, Greenwich (soon to be demolished), and the anti-racist mural in Woolwich Church Street are two examples of their work in South East London.

PYE, William. (b. 1938). An internationally acclaimed sculptor, best known to Londoners probably for his piece called Zemran outside the Queen Elizabeth Hall. His two water sculptures 'Slipstream' and 'Jetstream' at Gatwick Airport's new North Terminal received the Association of Business Sponsorship of the Arts Award in 1988 for the best commission of art in any medium. W.J. Strachen's book Open air sculpture in Britain contains information on other public pieces. He had a studio at Surrey Docks in the 1970's.

RECKITT, Rachel. (b. 1908). A wood engraver, she illustrated a number of books from 1945 to 1954. Her illustrations to Sam Price Myer's London South of the River, 1949 are especially attractive. Her work is, however, mainly figurative, rather than topographical. A more recent book is her Seven Psalms, 1981. In 1990 she exhibited with three other engravers at the Duncan Campbell Gallery, South Kensington.

RIZZELLO, Michael. (b. 1926). Internationally famous sculptor, who works in most sculptural media and at all scales from large architectural works, public statuary to wild-life sculpture, portrait busts, plaques, medals and coin design. He has designed coins for some 90 countries. Works in the U.K. include the memorial to David Lloyd George in Cardiff, the portrait bust of Sir Thomas Beecham, Royal Opera House, Covent Garden; portraits of Reginald M Phillips at the National Postal Museum, London, and Sussex University; statue of Sir William Sevenoke at Sevenoaks, Kent, a bronze fountain for Luton and Dunstable Hospital, aluminium sculptures for Sussex Square, London, and a portrait bust of Lord Stevens of Ludgate at Ludgate House. He was president of the Society of Portrait Sculptors 1968-73, and President of the Royal Society of British Sculptors 1976-1986.

SHEPHERD, Thomas Hosmer. Son of George Shepherd, his delicate, precise water-colour topographical drawings have been long admired. Frederick Crace (his important collection is now in the British Museum) commissioned him to draw many threatened buildings, especially old taverns and almshouses. Five of his East End almshouse drawings are reproduced in An East London Album (Peter Marcan Publications, 1992).

SOLOWAY, Louise. At a time when the world seems rather joyless, it is most heartening to discover an artist who can look at humanity with affection and amusement. She continues to find inspiration in the East End and some 20 of her recent drawings were recently exhibited at Whitechapel Library. She has also been making forays into the City, and has carried out two fibreglass relief Commissions: in 1991 of LIFFE ('Crazy Liffe'), and in 1992 (from Johannes Linhart) of the trading room of UBS Phillips & Drew ('Worlds Apart'). The three drawings featured were especially commissioned for this publication. Three other drawings of her's were published in A London Docklands Album (Peter Marcan Publications, 1990), and a photograph of her Oxford House, Bethnal Green fibre glass relief forms the frontispiece to An East London Album (Peter Marcan Publications, 1992).

WASHINGTON, William. (1885-1956). Painter, and line engraver of architectural views, portraits and figure subjects. He taught at Southend and Clapham Art Schools and was head of the Department of Arts and Craft at Hammersmith. The Guildhall Library holds a number of his engravings of other Central London subjects.

WAY, Thomas Robert. (1861-193). Important artist in the revival of lithography in Britain. He taught the medium to Whistler in 1978 and they became intimate friends, writing a book on the artist in 1903.

WILLIAMS, Hubert. (1905-1989). Studied at the Royal Academy Schools 1927-1932. He became a freelance artist drawing London architecture and street scenes, and his drawings were published in the Daily Chronicle, the Observer, The Times, and Blue Peter Magazine. He later undertook much portraiture and illustrated children's books. For the last twenty years of his life he lived in Cheltenham concentrating on portraiture and flower painting. His work is in a number of public collections including Westminster City Libraries, the South London Art Gallery, the Museum of London, and the Guildhall. His drawing of the Spa Road municipal buildings (before war damage) is used in a number of editions of the Bermondsey Official Guide.

ZIEGLER, Helen. (b. 1965). The lino print of Tower Bridge reproduced is not typical of this artist's work (submitted as a result of an appeal notice for Tower Bridge images in Artists Newsletter). Her themes stem from African and other ethnic art: people, animals and patterns painted and printed simply. She studied at the City and Guilds of London Art School. Students there, she tells me, are often taken to draw at Tower Bridge. She is a versatile, energetic individual, and through the 1980's has worked for a variety of business, charitable, and educational organisations.

ADVERTS

THE BITTER CRY HEARD AND HEEDED:
the story of the
South London Mission
1889-1989;
by John D. Beasley; forward by
Lord Soper. Available, price £6
from Bermondsey Central Hall,
Bermondsey St, London SE1 3UJ

WELCOME!

to the new

TEA AND COFFEE MUSEUM

Located in the
CLOVE BUILDING
Maguire Street, SE1

(By The Design Museum)

Open 10.00-6.00pm

071 378 0222

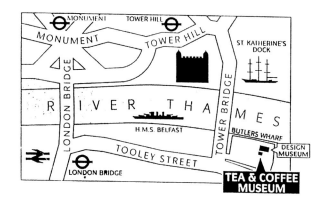